Global Wikipedia

Global Wikipedia

International and Cross-Cultural Issues in Online Collaboration

Edited by Pnina Fichman and Noriko Hara

ROWMAN & LITTLEFIELD
Lanham • Boulder • New York • Toronto • Plymouth, UK

Published by Rowman & Littlefield
4501 Forbes Boulevard, Suite 200, Lanham, Maryland 20706
www.rowman.com

10 Thornbury Road, Plymouth PL6 7PP, United Kingdom

British Library Cataloguing in Publication Information Available

Library of Congress Cataloging-in-Publication Data

Global Wikipedia : international and cross-cultural issues in online collaboration / Edited by Pnina Fichman and Noriko Hara.
    pages cm
  Includes bibliographical references and index.
  ISBN 978-0-8108-9101-2 (cloth : alk. paper) — ISBN 978-0-8108-9102-9 (electronic)
  1. Wikipedia. 2. User-generated content—Cross-cultural studies. 3. Electronic encyclopedias—Cross-cultural studies. 4. Multilingualism—Data processing. 5. Language and culture—Data processing. I. Fichman, Pnina. II. Hara, Noriko, 1971-
  ZA4482.G56 2014
  030—dc23

                                                          2014003495

♾™ The paper used in this publication meets the minimum requirements of American National Standard for Information Sciences—Permanence of Paper for Printed Library Materials, ANSI/NISO Z39.48-1992.

Printed in the United States of America

Contents

List of Figures

List of Tables

Acknowledgment

This book was made possible through the contributions of many individuals. First, we thank each of the contributors who authored or coauthored the chapters in this edited volume; their invaluable contributions enhanced our understanding of the global nature of Wikipedia. In addition, we are very grateful for the superb assistance from Jylisa Doney, whose editorial skills were crucial in making this entire publication what it had become. We are also thankful to John McCurley for providing valuable editorial comments. Finally, we are indebted to Charles Harmon for his initiative, support, and timely help at various stages of the publication of this book.

Introduction

Pnina Fichman and Noriko Hara

This book focuses attention on the global nature of Wikipedia, providing an international and cross-cultural perspective on various sociotechnical aspects of the Wikipedia project, such as conflict and collaboration, neutrality of viewpoint, and the gender gap in contributions. While Wikipedia is the focus of extensive scholarly and popular media attention, our book is unique in that it provides an important global perspective on this endeavor to accumulate massive amounts of knowledge. A global perspective on Wikipedia is needed, because more than 80 percent of Wikipedia is written in languages other than English; these different language versions of Wikipedia represent contributors from various countries with diverse sociocultural, political, and religious beliefs. Furthermore, the English Wikipedia itself attracts users from all over the world, which involves intercultural collaborative processes of knowledge production. This global nature of Wikipedia offers a rich sociotechnical environment to investigate a wide range of international and cross-cultural issues online. It is somewhat surprising that despite the global reach of Wikipedia, much of the literature has examined primarily the English version of Wikipedia. To address this lacuna we compiled this edited volume that examines the global and multilingual nature of Wikipedia, its cross-cultural variations, and the international cooperation it fosters. We chose chapters that include comparative studies of Wikipedia in more than one language and case studies of Wikipedia in languages other than English.

With a special interest in taking a sociotechnical approach to Wikipedia research, these chapters focus on content, processes, structures, and policies of Wikipedia. After all, Wikipedia is a sociotechnical system: a system of interactions between people and technology, dependent on both humans and machines. On one side, Wikipedia is based on a system invented and named by Ward Cunningham in 1994 called *wiki*, the Hawaiian term synonymous with "quick" in English.[1] The wiki system allows multiple users to edit documents easily and collaboratively. Additionally, as described in Randall Livingstone's chapter, bots play major roles in constructing knowledge in Wikipedia. On the other side of the system, volunteers, users, and administrators contribute content, policies, structures, and interactions. These coexist and coevolve alongside the technologies, as they mutually shape each other. This collaboration between social and technical components in Wikipedia makes it a unique sociotechnical system to analyze.

Because this edited volume approaches Wikipedia as a sociotechnical system, it showcases context-sensitive studies that examine the manifestation of international and cross-cultural issues. The selected chapters highlight: 1) international collaboration and controversy that cross language boundaries; 2) the gender gap in Wikipedia contribution; 3) neutrality of viewpoint in global and multilingual contexts; and 4) the exhibition of corporate interests.

Collaboration and controversy in Wikipedia have been the primary issues of attention for Wikipedia scholars (e.g., Viégas, Wattenberg, and Dave 2004). However, much of this early work focused on the English Wikipedia. Expanding these issues into the multicultural, multilingual, global setting of Wikipedia, two chapters focus on global cooperation and two on conflict and controversy. Focusing on global cooperation, Livingstone's "Immaterial Editors: Bots and Bot Policies across Global Wikipedia" and Pnina Fichman and Noriko Hara's "Knowledge Sharing on Wikimedia Embassies," present how collaboration between users from various parts of the world occurs on Wikipedia. The former chapter takes a sociotechnical approach to the development, use, and maintenance of Wikipedia bots on a global scale. The latter examines knowledge-sharing practices in terms of the content and style of online exchanges found on twenty-one Wikimedia embassies. Controversy and conflict on Wikipedia is the focus of two other chapters in this book. The first of the two, "The Most Controversial Topics in Wikipedia: A Multilingual and Geographic Analysis" by Taha Yasseri, Anselm Spoerri, Mark Graham, and János Kertész, takes a global approach by identifying the most controversial topics on ten language versions of Wikipedia. The authors found that politics and religion dominate the list of the most controversial topics. They then argue that Wikipedia is not only an encyclopedia but also a window into convergent and divergent social-spatial priorities, interests, and preferences. Likewise, the second of these chapters, "The Copycat of Wikipedia in China" by Gehao Zhang, demonstrates how sociopolitical and economic factors impact the two major Chinese copycats of Wikipedia. From a sociotechnical point of view, the case study demonstrates delicate processes through which local, global, social, technological, economical, and political forces impact the content of Wikipedia and its Chinese copycats.

The gender gap is a persistent issue with regard to Wikipedia contributions, as men and women do not contribute equally to Wikipedia. Jimmy Wales, the founder of Wikipedia, stated that men contribute 87 percent of all contributions to Wikipedia (Zara 2013). This pattern of male-dominant contributions skews the content to cover more articles on male-oriented topics. Efforts to address this problem include, for example, the so-called Edit-a-Thon, an initiative by the Royal Society in the

United Kingdom to contribute more about women scientists on Wikipedia and to increase their recognition (Yong 2012). Two chapters in this book focus attention on the gender gap from two different perspectives. In "Gender Gap in Wikipedia Editing: A Cross Language Comparison," authors Paolo Massa and Asta Zelenkauskaite take a global approach to the gender gap and examine the gender distribution of users in seventy-six different language versions of Wikipedia. They found that while in all languages the majority of the contributors are male, female contributors range from 4 percent to 40 percent of all contributions in different language versions of Wikipedia. The authors note that the Wikipedia online system reflects differences in women participation in public life in general and science in particular. Building on this idea, in the second chapter, "Contributing to Wikipedia: A Question of Gender" by Hélène Bourdeloie and Michaël Vicente, the authors demonstrate and explain how Wikipedia, despite its potential to bridge the gender gap, in fact creates and maintains a system of gender inequality.

Neutral point of view (NPOV) is one of the fundamental policies that Wikipedia has encouraged contributors to follow from the beginning. Originally, Jimmy Wales and Larry Sanger made this rule to prohibit people from taking any positions about specific articles.[2] They insisted that if Wikipedia was to become a successful online encyclopedia, then articles should be unbiased. When disagreement arises, contributors are encouraged to discuss their opinions on the discussion pages that are attached to every single article (Poe 2006). Maintaining NPOV is easier said than done. Yasseri and his colleagues in their chapter, "The Most Controversial Topics in Wikipedia: A Multilingual and Geographic Analysis," examined and analyzed the similarities and differences in the "edit wars" of controversial topics within ten different Wikipedia language versions that were grouped into three language groups. They discovered that some topics, such as Israel, Hitler, the Holocaust, and God, are highly contested in each of the three language groups, and concluded that numerous controversial articles appear on Wikipedia, including articles related to religion and politics. As such, NPOV became one of the most debated policies in Wikipedia (Nagar 2012). Naturally, when we expand beyond the scope of the English-language Wikipedia, NPOV lends itself to a wide range of interpretations. Two chapters from this book, Ewa Callahan's "Crosslinguistic Neutrality: Wikipedia's Neutral Points of View from a Global Perspective" and Jahna Otterbacher's "Our News, Their Events? A Comparison of Archived Current Events on English and Greek Wikipedias," touch on NPOV policies and perspectives. Callahan's chapter compares NPOV from fifteen different language versions of Wikipedia. Languages were split into three groups: regional languages, national languages, and local languages. A more detailed analysis of the Polish-language Wikipedia and its Talk pages was conducted to learn more about NPOV policy development. Callahan concludes that even though NPOV policies are different among Wikipedia language versions, these differences do not mean that neutrality is unimportant in these cultures. Instead, these concepts may be viewed as ambiguous or based on other types of cultural understanding. Otterbacher compared the archived current events portals of the English and Greek

Wikipedias to determine the relationships between a global repository (English) and a more regional Wikipedia (Greek). She identified similarities and differences in the coverage of international events and concluded that the current events portals in smaller Wikipedias are especially important, because they can transmit international news to a regional audience in a meaningful way and engage citizens in local news issues.

Corporate interests and impacts on Wikipedia content increase as Wikipedia grows to be one of the top-ten most visited websites.[3] Corporations have begun to pay more attention to the articles about them posted on Wikipedia. This online content shapes corporate reputation among the general public and can impact the success or failure of individual corporations. Consequently, some corporations attempt to manipulate such web content. For example, a public relations firm, Bell Pottinger, has edited English Wikipedia articles for their clients to reflect positive images of these companies (Lee 2011). Subsequently, the account links to Bell Pottinger were suspended because this kind of behavior violates Wikipedia's conflict-of-interest policy. This is not the only incident reported in regard to corporate interests and Wikipedia content. In order to make these activities transparent, the Wikipedia Scanner was developed to identify users' affiliations based on contributors' IP addresses (Borland 2007). Two chapters address corporate interests in Wikipedia: Salla-Maaria Laaksonen and Merja Porttikivi's "Constructing Local Heroes: Collaborative Narratives of Finnish Corporations in Wikipedia" and Gehao Zhang's "The Copycat of Wikipedia in China." Laaksonen and Porttikivi's chapter investigates how narratives were formed in the Finnish Wikipedia by analyzing the articles for the top one hundred Finnish companies. They selected a total of fourteen cases that represented conflicts of interest for more detailed analysis. Over time, the type of narrative units of these fourteen corporate entries maintained a similar structure. Additionally, corporate interests are not only limited to the content of Wikipedia but also include capitalization of Wikipedia-like websites. "The Copycat of Wikipedia in China" introduces an intriguing case study of Wikipedia copycats. To pursue corporate profits, some Chinese companies decided to duplicate Wikipedia in a politically restrained regime, which gave rise to two copycats of Wikipedia. These two Chinese copycats exemplify a type of social factory in which, according to Zhang, contributions are exploited. The Chinese Wikipedia copycats operate in a manner almost completely opposite of what Wikipedia strives for—free access to information.

These nine chapters shed light on the global nature of Wikipedia and at the same time highlight many possibilities for future research. First and foremost, it is clear that it would be beneficial to conduct and publish more studies that deal with cross-cultural issues and to provide a global scope to a wide range of significant issues in Wikipedia, such as vandalism. Because many existing studies are limited in their samples, increasing sample size to include more language versions of Wikipedia in any given study may enhance our knowledge of Wikipedia as a whole. Investigation of smaller Wikipedias, such as Twi Wikipedia (used in Ghana) and Kongo Wikipedia, or minority-language Wikipedias, such as Welsh Wikipedia and Hawaiian Wikipedia, may increase our understanding of the developmental patterns of content, structure, policies, and interactions. Likewise, more longitudinal studies could provide more comprehensive understanding of intercultural and cross-cultural dynamics in various Wikipedias. While the studies included in this volume primarily collect data from readily available online content and thus are limited in scope, the next step is to interview users and system administrators to shed light on the global nature of Wikipedia. Finally, comparing Wikipedia with other social media sites is important, as we have limited understanding of whether the cultural differences and language sensitivity found in the physical space would directly transfer to Web 2.0 environments and how it could possibly vary further by specific context and the attributes of its communities.

NOTES

1. History of Wikis, http://en.wikipedia.org/wiki/History_of_wikis.
2. User: Larry Sanger/Origins of Wikipedia, http://en.wikipedia.org/wiki/User:Larry_Sanger/Origins_of_Wikipedia#Wasn.27t_Jimmy_Wales_responsible_for_the_.22neutral_point_of_view.22_policy.3F_Didn.27t_you_oppose_it.3F.
3. Top 5 Most Popular Websites, ebizmba.com, http://www.ebizmba.com/articles/most-popular-websites.

REFERENCES

Borland, John. "See Who's Editing Wikipedia—Diebold, the CIA, a Campaign." *Wired*, August 14, 2007. http://www.wired.com/politics/onlinerights/news/2007/08/wiki_tracker?currentPage=all.

Lee, Dave. "Wikipedia Investigates PR Firm Bell Pottinger's Edits." *BBC*, December 8, 2011. http://www.bbc.co.uk/news/technology-16084861.

Nagar, Yiftach. "What Do You Think? The Structuring of an Online Community as a Collective-Sensemaking Process." Proceedings of the 2012 Annual Conference on Computer Supported Cooperative Work, Seattle, Washington, February 11–15, 2012.

Poe, Marshall. "The Hive." *The Atlantic*, September 1, 2006. http://www.theatlantic.com/magazine/archive/2006/09/the-hive/305118/.

Viégas, Fernanda B., Martin Wattenberg, and Kushal Dave. "Studying Cooperation and Conflict between Authors with *History Flow* Visualizations." ACM *CHI 2004*, Vienna, Austria, April 24–29, 2004. http://alumni.media.mit.edu/~fviegas/papers/history_flow.pdf.

Yong, Ed. "Edit-a-Thon Gets Women Scientists into Wikipedia: Royal Society Hosts Event to Address Online Encyclopaedia's Gender Imbalance." *Nature*, October 22, 2012. http://www.nature.com/news/edit-a-thon-gets-women-scientists-into-wikipedia-1.11636.

Zara, Christopher. "Wikipedia's Gender Gap Persists: Why Don't More Women Contribute to the Online Encyclopedia?" *International Business Times*, August 19, 2013. http://www.ibtimes.com/wikipedias-gender-gap-persists-why-dont-more-women-contribute-online-encyclopedia-1390565.

1

Immaterial Editors

Bots and Bot Policies across Global Wikipedia

Randall Livingstone

In the online lexicon, the term *meatbot* is hacker slang for a warm-blooded machine (i.e., a human being).[1] Slightly pejorative, the irony of the moniker comes from the fact that technology is the central frame of reference for the term, not humanity. Meatbots are an extension of their computing, not the other way around. The meatbot's foil is the software robot, or "bot," a program or script that carries out an often tedious or repetitive task for its creator. Bots are written to operate largely unsupervised and "without the necessity of human decision-making,"[2] and therein lies the joke; meatbots operate like unthinking machines.

While *meatbot* is not a widely used term on Wikipedia, the English-language version does contain the shortcut WP:MEATBOTS, which redirects to the subsection of its Bot Policy named "bot-like editing." The policy reads:

> Human editors are expected to pay attention to the edits they make, and ensure that they don't sacrifice quality in the pursuit of speed or quantity. For the purpose of dispute resolution, it is irrelevant whether high-speed or large-scale edits that involve errors an attentive human would not make are actually being performed by a bot, by a human assisted by a script, or even by a human without any programmatic assistance.[3]

As such, assisted-editing tasks that mimic bot editing in terms of speed or scope should go through the same review process as any fully automated bot task would. More conceptually, however, this particular policy points to the vastly sociotechnical nature of the work being done on Wikipedia. Here, "for the purpose of dispute resolution"—a very social sphere of the project—meatbots and software bots are the same.

While a vast amount of academic literature on Wikipedia has appeared in the past decade, including some from a sociotechnical perspective, only a few studies have explored the sociotechnical implications of bots on the site.[4] Yet as Niederer and van Dijck call attention to,[5] the sheer amount of raw work that bots carry out across most language versions of the project deserves closer inspection and analysis, especially if we hope to understand how the collaborative work on Wikipedia bridges both social/technical and language/culture gaps. We know that different language versions of the project are autonomous in many ways, self-determining policies, processes, standards, and etiquette—the things that make each a local culture and community. And yet each version is a piece in a larger enterprise, guided by the same overarching goals of free knowledge, consensus decision making, and good-faith collaboration.[6] Many Wikipedia bots and those who operate them parallel this dualism, often negotiating both local and global interests in order to perform tasks that range from simple template maintenance to advanced vandalism detection, interwiki linking to enforcing user protocol, and on some language versions, even new article creation. Bots have contributed to nearly all of the 285 language versions of Wikipedia, and yet, as a distinct user class in the MediaWiki software, their edits do not appear in Recent Changes feeds. These are mostly silent and unseen actors indubitably important for the health and growth of the project.

On the surface, bots may seem to be a purely technical species, coded by Wikipedian programmers (usually in Python) to carry out tedious, algorithmic tasks. But experience on the site reveals they are much more—they are actors in sociotechnical ecosystems very much informed by and imbued with the culture of their environment. Both the recent plateau of human contributors to Wikipedia and the creation of Wikidata, a centralized data repository for all language versions, highlight the evolving significance (if not prominence) of bots on the site today and moving forward.

This chapter explores the sociotechnical nature of the global Wikipedia by looking more closely at how the historical trajectory and present status of bots on various language versions have been shaped by local policies and policymakers, and how this programmed population of editors might adapt to the recent global initiative to centralize data on the project. After a brief description of this research's methodology, the chapter begins by exploring the definition of bots both concretely and conceptually. A concise history of bots on Wikipedia is then presented, from the controversial work of the first mass-editing bot, rambot, in 2002, to the spread of bots across language versions and the development of the global bot flag. The current state of bots across language versions is examined, using data from early 2013, and current bot policies and the local communities that create and manage them are investigated to highlight similarities and differences across language versions. Finally, the implications of bot work, both local and global, are discussed in light of both fragmented and holistic perceptions of Wikipedia moving forward.

METHODOLOGY

Data presented in this chapter is drawn from my ongoing research on Wikipedia bots, bot operators, and the site's technical community and infrastructure. Two main research methods are used in this work: document analysis and semistructured interviewing. These methods complement each other when used to study Wikipedia, as archived Talk pages and page histories often reveal valuable potential interviewees, while the interviewees in turn regularly refer to relevant documents and discussions tucked away in the site's massive archives. Following these leads produces a snowball sample of both documents and interviews that inform the overall research project.

To examine the structure and content of bot policies across language versions of Wikipedia, a more purposive sample of documents was selected for this inquiry. Bot policies and/or regulations were located on the twenty-five language versions with the largest bot populations. On some projects, all policies are contained on one wiki page, while others have relevant information spread between a policy page and a bot request-for-approval page. All pertinent documents were located and analyzed for similarities, differences, and unique features using a note-taking software package. Many language versions include an English translation of key information, but generally this is only a subset of the full policy. Therefore, all non-English policies were translated using Google Translate before analysis. Any questions regarding translated terms or language were clarified during the interview process.

Interviewing was conducted in two stages. First, a convenience sample was drawn from the operators of the most active (by number of edits) English Wikipedia and interwiki bots. Next, another convenience sample was drawn from editors actively involved in bot approvals on the twenty-five language versions with the largest bot populations. A total of fifty-six interviews were conducted, mostly via Internet Relay Chat (IRC).

Finally, statistical data used in this project was gathered in two ways. Data on bot registrations and bot edits was scraped from a static version of the site residing on the Wikimedia Toolserver by English Wikipedia User Madman on February 19, 2013, and analyzed by the author. Data on total Wikipedia users, total edits, and number of articles was procured on the same date from Wikimedia's live List of Wikipedias page.[7]

IMMATERIAL ACTORS: DEFINING BOTS

MetaWiki, the global community site for all of Wikimedia's projects, defines a bot as "a robot designed for performing certain repetitive tasks on a wiki."[8] Bots are certainly not unique to wikis, though. Whether enforcing protocols on Internet Relay Chat (IRC) channels, scouring the Web for search engines such as Google, or interacting with your Second Life avatar, bots are constantly active in almost all areas of the Internet. As Andrew Leonard accounts in *Bots: The Origin of New Species*, the history of bots stretches back to MIT in the early 1960s, where Dr. Fernando Corbató programmed the first script to run autonomously on a local time-sharing network.[9] Soon after, chatterbots like ELIZA, programs designed to process natural language and simulate human conversation, were developed and eventually released into networked environments like MUDs (Multi-User Dungeon) and MOOs (MUD object oriented) in the 1980s and 1990s.[10] Today, bots are perhaps best known to the general Internet user base for one of their more disruptive uses: spambots.

A bot is in essence an immaterial actor—the Swedish Wikipedia describes it as "a soulless thing"[11]—lines of computer code that form a script to carry out an algorithmic task. Wikipedia bots are largely written in the Python programming language, and developers on the site have created a collection of tools known as *pywikipediabot* (shorthand for Python Wikipediabot Framework) from which many bots are built. This is not part of the MediaWiki software package that Wikipedia is run on, though, and bots do not extend the core functionality of that software as MediaWiki Extensions do. Bots are separate programmed entities, often interacting with the site in a similar manner to human editors—from user accounts. Bots receive the same user namespace and Talk page as any other account, and some bot operators choose to anthropomorphize their bots through images, photos, or first-person descriptions (figure 1.1). On Talk pages, British User Noommos noted, "I've often encountered users trying to talk to a bot." Of course, it is the bot operator who would ultimately reply, but these parallels underscore the sociotechnical nature of participating on the site. The English Wikipedia even allows certain bots to have administrative rights (adminbots), including the ability to block users and delete pages. And although most bot operators discuss their bots as simple programs to get tasks done, in many ways, bots represent much more than their lines of code—they represent a significant population of influence in a sociotechnical network of actors.

R. Stuart Geiger, in his "The Lives of Bots," traces the politics of this influence through two controversies on the English Wikipedia: a bot's potential election to the Arbitration Committee and another's conflict with human editors over signing unsigned comments.[12] In his assessment of these episodes, Gieger argues that bots "already have a similar level of influence [to human editors] on how Wikipedia as a free and open encyclopedia project is constituted. However . . . bots are also subject to social and political pressures, and we must be careful to not fall into familiar narratives of technological determinism when asking who—or what—actually controls Wikipedia."[13] To do this, actor-network theory (ANT), a sociological approach developed by Bruno Latour and Michel Callon to understand influence in social networks,[14] helps us understand the work of bots in this sociotechnical context; here, they are more than just tools, but truly autonomous or semiautonomous agents in a system. Latour argues that "in order to understand domination we have to turn away from an exclusive concern with social relations and weave them into a fabric that includes non-human actants, actants that offer the possibility of holding society together as a durable whole."[15] ANT also advises that we "follow the actors" in such a network, as combinations of agents, human or otherwise, are constantly binding together and breaking apart as power relations shift.[16]

Indeed, on Wikipedia, a project in perpetual motion, human-bot relationships are consistently changing. New bots are developed to relieve the greater community of certain tasks, but on most of the larger language versions, the consensus process of approval—a deeply social cornerstone to the Wikipedia community—mitigates their

Figure 1.1.   Example of a bot user page.

introduction. Even once approved, some communities experience controversies, such as those highlighted by Geiger, when actors shift position in such a network. ANT asks us to avoid privileging human actors in these controversies, as all actors in the network of relations are inscribed with the meanings and beliefs of the culture. Disputes around the allowances and behaviors of bots are particularly determined by what the local community believes a bot should or should not be allowed to do. Many language versions prohibit bots from creating new articles or correcting spelling issues, as these tasks are deemed only appropriate for human discretion, while others (Dutch, Arabic) sometimes feel this work can benefit their project. Both these beliefs and their implications for bots can and do shift over time (as ANT would predict), opening up and closing off possibilities for Wikipedia to evolve. Indeed, the idea that code and computer algorithms need to be understood for more than their surface-level utility, and therefore explored with a more inclusive, liberal, and sociotechnical analysis, is driving much recent, important work in digital media studies[17] and offers new, dynamic perspectives for understanding bot work on Wikipedia.

ORIGIN AND PROLIFERATION OF BOTS ON WIKIPEDIA

The first bots appeared on Wikipedia in late 2001, less than a year after the project's founding, but it was in 2002 that bots began to stir serious discussions on the site. Without any regulations or policies in place, English User Ram-Man decided to "be bold" and automate the process for creating articles for each city and town in the United States. Over the course of approximately one week in December 2002, his rambot created over thirty thousand new articles for the project, populating each with data culled from the U.S. Census Bureau and the CIA World Factbook websites. The result was an expansion of the English-language version by 60 percent, as well as the flooding of its Recent Changes feed and many individual watchlists. Discussions along both technical (slowing down the MediaWiki servers) and substantive (inclusionist/deletionist debates) lines emerged from the rambot's work, and an official bot policy page for the English Wikipedia was soon developed by Ram-Man and other early technical contributors to the project.[18]

The historical records for when bots first edited other languages are buried deep in the discussion pages and archived lists of local projects; these sources suggest limited bot work as early as 2003 on other large versions, including French and German.[19] Some bots operated in the open with community support, while others may have run inconspicuously at slow speeds from ordinary user accounts. But with the release of MediaWiki version 1.5 in October 2005, which established "bot" as a distinct user group with its own privileges, came a proliferation of bots across Wikipedia. By January 2006, fifty-four language versions had registered bots, as well as some versions of Wiktionary, Wikisource, and Wikinews; by January 2007, these figures rose to 245 language versions and 471 other Wikimedia projects. As of this writing (March 2013), 273 language versions of Wikipedia (95.8 percent) have at least one registered bot.

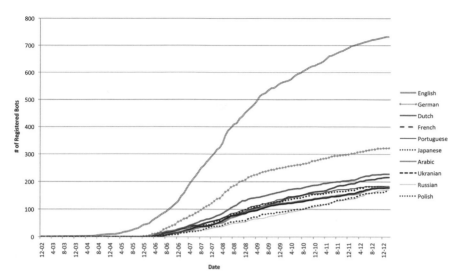

Figure 1.2. Ten largest bot populations on Wikipedia language versions.

Growth over time of the registered bot populations on many of the larger language versions (by number of articles) has been steady (figure 1.2). The English Wikipedia has the most registered bots (732) by far, more than twice the amount of the German Wikipedia (322). Overall, twenty-six language versions have registered bot populations over one hundred. Compared to the total registered users on these projects, however, these numbers are miniscule, representing a fraction of a percent of the overall user base on each (table 1.1). Furthermore, many bots are registered on numerous projects and are not unique to local Wikipedias (a fact explored in more depth in the next section).

As Niederer and van Dijck point out in their earlier study, the more significant statistics for understanding the role of bots on Wikipedia may be the massive volume of edits they are carrying out.[20] Across all language versions, bot edits account for 24.8 percent of all edits made to the site.[21] This proportion is lower for some of the larger projects (for example, English, German, and Spanish), but for the majority of language versions, including some large projects (Dutch, Polish, Portuguese), a quarter or more of their edits are made from bot accounts (table 1.2). For some midsized projects like Basque, Lithuanian, and Slovenian, bots have made closer to half of all edits, while for many smaller language versions, this percentage rises as high as 75 percent (table 1.2).

GLOBAL BOTS

While the size of individual bot populations and the volume of edits by bots on Wikipedia give us a sense of the scope of work being carried out by these automated

Table 1.1. Twenty-Five Largest Bot Populations on Wikipedia

	Registered Users					Edits					Size	
	Bots		Total Users		% Bot Users	Bot Edits		Total Edits		% Edits by Bots	Articles	
	Rank	#	Rank	#		Rank	#	Rank	#		Rank	#
English (en)	1	732	1	18574917	0.0039%	1	57597590	1	598664482	9.6210%	1	4181785
German (de)	2	322	3	1617485	0.0199%	3	12362611	2	120459830	10.2628%	2	1561118
Dutch (nl)	3	228	12	517111	0.0441%	5	11891835	8	36076035	32.9633%	4	1218293
French (fr)	4	216	4	1509780	0.0143%	2	20568200	3	89537388	22.9716%	3	1361863
Portuguese (pt)	5	184	6	1113842	0.0165%	6	10394741	10	35237609	29.4990%	11	772386
Japanese (ja)	6	182	9	713836	0.0255%	12	5421274	7	47534039	11.4050%	9	849118
Arabic (ar)	7	181	10	605202	0.0299%	16	4608772	18	12768807	36.0940%	25	217749
Ukrainian (uk)	8	178	27	169459	0.1050%	13	5211188	20	12160824	42.8523%	14	433951
Russian (ru)	9	171	7	1011704	0.0169%	7	9076439	6	60788789	14.9311%	6	977813
Polish (pl)	10	166	11	544192	0.0305%	8	9033866	9	35562159	25.4030%	8	955280
Danish (da)	11	162	26	182113	0.0890%	24	2870204	27	7223736	39.7330%	33	175915
Persian (fa)	12	159	15	332963	0.0478%	14	4916821	14	14039698	35.0208%	18	301404
Italian (it)	13	156	8	859662	0.0181%	4	12087478	5	62023957	19.4884%	5	1013725
Catalan (ca)	14	153	29	139175	0.1099%	15	4870473	22	11454229	42.5212%	15	396528
Hungarian (hu)	15	153	22	225036	0.0680%	17	4061806	15	13806341	29.4199%	22	235839
Turkish (tr)	16	150	13	464254	0.0323%	20	3460579	16	13791155	25.0927%	26	206229
Chinese (zh)	17	147	5	1385787	0.0106%	11	5584144	11	26340917	21.1995%	12	678473
Romanian (ro)	18	145	20	252921	0.0573%	18	3555628	25	7799813	45.5861%	24	224205
Spanish (es)	19	138	2	2551237	0.0054%	9	8090837	4	69473281	11.6460%	7	975432
Esperanto (eo)	20	136	38	80170	0.1696%	25	2720321	31	5095925	53.3823%	32	176970
Serbian (sr)	21	131	32	119322	0.1098%	19	3491217	28	7118360	49.0452%	30	183071
Slovenian (sl)	22	127	35	107074	0.1186%	30	2069703	34	4051768	51.0815%	38	136493
Indonesian (id)	23	123	14	443390	0.0277%	22	3125166	26	7477052	41.7968%	27	205874
Slovak (sk)	24	120	36	86019	0.1395%	26	2641350	30	5272899	50.0929%	31	182120
Vietnamese (vi)	25	117	16	322544	0.0363%	10	6538644	23	10504372	62.2469%	13	577261

Source: Bot data aggregated from Wikimedia Toolserver on February 19, 2013, by User Madman. Total users, edits, and articles data retrieved from List of Wikipedias, http//meta.wikimedia.org/wiki/List_of_Wikipedias.

Table 1.2. Ten Language Versions with High Percentage of Bot Edits

	Bots		Registered Users			Edits					Size	
			Total Users		%	Bot Edits		Total Edits		% Edits	Articles	
	Rank	#	Rank	#	Bot Users	Rank	#	Rank	#	by Bots	Rank	#
Volapük (vo)	31	95	89	15795	0.6015%	28	2403552	40	3180226	75.5780%	40	119091
Low Saxon (nds)	69	61	122	9393	0.6494%	69	474307	85	715498	66.2905%	145	5075
Swahili (sw)	34	93	92	15050	0.6179%	65	615262	74	928650	66.2534%	84	25186
Bengali (bn)	31	96	55	43025	0.2231%	49	926452	65	1444440	64.1420%	83	25632
Bashkir (ba)	76	55	138	7736	0.7110%	92	242743	107	381995	63.5461%	76	30274
Venetian (vec)	55	77	107	10992	0.7005%	84	338031	95	548283	61.6527%	120	9958
Breton (br)	58	76	68	25796	0.2946%	50	908551	63	1518321	59.8392%	65	45276
Cebuano (ceb)	71	57	99	12569	0.4535%	46	1167058	53	2006176	58.1733%	19	273315
Aragonese (an)	55	77	67	26243	0.2934%	52	889982	62	1537312	57.8921%	78	29078
Luxembourgish (lb)	29	101	76	20806	0.4854%	54	857240	60	1579646	54.2679%	71	38258

Source: Bot data aggregated from Wikimedia Toolserver on February 19, 2013, by User Madman. Total users, edits, and articles data retrieved from List of Wikipedias, http://meta.wikimedia.org/wiki/List_of_Wikipedias.

programs, these statistics do not tell us some of the important details and nuances of bots on the site, and in some ways even overexaggerate the role of bots on local projects. For example, the Russian Wikipedia has 171 registered bot accounts, but as User Rubin16, author of the Russian Wikipedia's Bot Policy, points out, only "10 to 20 bots perform unique tasks that are really helpful" for local editors. Bot operators from the Dutch, Spanish, and Portuguese projects report a similar reality. So what are the rest of these registered bots doing? Most are carrying out tasks that fall under the moniker of "interwiki linking."

Links are a core element to the wiki concept originally developed by Ward Cunningham and outlined in his coauthored book (with Bo Leuf) *The Wiki Way*: "Wiki promotes meaningful topic associations between different pages by making page link creation almost intuitively easy."[22] However, as Wikipedia grew to hundreds of thousands of articles across dozens of projects, technical contributors realized "it is a challenge to maintain the links from an article in one language to all of the versions of that article in other languages. Each time a new version is introduced, changes name, or is deleted, all of the other versions should be updated."[23] To tackle the challenge, interwiki bots were designed to handle this continuous, often tedious, and time-intensive flood of work.

An additional hurdle emerged as these contributors set out to use their bots, though. Unlike a human user, who can sign up for an account on any Wikipedia and begin editing immediately, bot accounts require a bureaucrat-granted flag, and many language versions either require a trial and discussion period before this flag is granted or are so small as to not have local bureaucrats, in which case Wikimedia stewards act on their behalf. Steward Pathoschild recounts:

> As interwiki bots became more common, they also became a major pain point for stewards: each interwiki bot wanted to run on hundreds of wikis, each of which had its own policies for approval. A single bot could take weeks of work from both the operator and stewards to approve.

The solution here was a Global Bot Policy, developed in September 2007 and housed on the Wikimedia Meta site. Global bots would be restricted to only maintaining interlanguage links or fixing linking problems.[24] To avoid discontent by local communities weary of a policy outside their own control, the policy is opt-in, allowing those communities to handle local bot requests themselves. Some 244 language versions have opted-in for global bots at the time of this writing.[25]

The existence of interwiki bots explains the high percentage of overall bot edits on many Wikipedias. For example, if we look at the bot activity on the Bashkir Wikipedia,[26] a project in which bot activity accounts for 63.5 percent of the overall edits, fifty-five total bots are registered, forty-three of which are interwiki bots. One of these, SieBot, has edited 260 language versions for a total of nearly ten million edits. In fact, despite the minor fanfare in 2012 surrounding English User koavf, the first contributor to reach one million edits,[27] forty-four interwiki bots have also passed that milestone, including two bots—EmausBot and Luckas-bot[28]—that have surpassed thirteen million edits each.

BOT POLICIES AND PROCEDURES

As the first Wikipedia to institutionalize bots, the English-language version's Bot Policy is the oldest and most edited page related to bots on the site. Some 688 users have edited the page since it was created by Ram-Man in October 2002, including (fittingly enough) thirty-eight bots.[29] The English Bot Policy is also the longest on Wikipedia and has been used as a model by several other languages. Russian and Arabic, for example, both projects with large registered bot populations, have adopted policy language directly from the English policy, tailored in spots to fit their local community. Similarly, the Meta Bot Policy serves as a reference point for other local policies. In recognition of the large amount of work carried out by foreign interwiki bots created by U.S. or European editors, many local projects provide an English translation of their bot policy, and specifically the rules and guidelines for global and interwiki bots. Dutch, Arabic, Norwegian (Bokmål), Slovenian, Russian, Finnish, and Danish all provide such sections on their policy pages.

Bot policies vary in length, but there are common elements that appear in most. A definition of "bot" is usually presented at the beginning of the policy, followed by a section on rules, regulations, and guidelines (figure 1.3). Defined here are basics on the setup and use of a bot account. To more easily identify these accounts on the user-viewed front end (as the bot flag is used for identification on the MediaWiki back end), all Wikipedias require that "bot" be a part of the account name; generally, this appears at the end of the name, as in SieBot or Addbot, and "bot" is almost globally used instead of translations of the term. Other common elements of bot policies include the speed at which a bot may edit, the tasks a bot should not carry out, and the expectations around communication from the bot operator.

The bot approval process is one of the biggest distinguishing factors between bot policies and bot communities across language versions of Wikipedia (as well as projects like Commons), and the method of approval speaks to the culture of bots on

Figure 1.3.   Requirements of a bot from Italian Bot Policy.

local projects. One of three major processes is generally used: a bureaucrat review, a broader community review, or an approvals group review.

As only local bureaucrats or Wikimedia stewards can grant the bot flag necessary to operate an authorized bot account, the simplest method is to appeal directly to these individuals. In the early years of Wikipedia bots, before more fully formed bot policies were established on some of the larger language versions, bot flags were granted in this manner. Contradictory to the project's ethos of community-driven consensus decision making and transparency, though, this simple process irked some editors, who called for at least a minimal review process by the community. Today, mainly small or new language versions of the project operate with only a bureaucrat review, which in practice is rare because a) many of these projects have no local bots, only interwiki or global bots who edit with a recognized global bot flag, and/or b) many of these projects have no local bureaucrats, thus requiring a steward to review the bot's proposed work.

A community review process is the most common method for approving bots on Wikipedia. On a local page created for the purpose of bot reviews, the author of a new bot is asked to post basic information about himself or herself, about the bot's script (often the programming language or framework used, and a list of other projects the bot is already approved on), and about the proposed task(s) to be carried out. On some language versions, a voting system of approval is set up with a required minimum threshold of support; for example, the French Wikipedia requires at least 75 percent of voters, who themselves must meet certain participation requirements, to support a bot's candidacy.[30] Other language versions, such as Russian and Finnish, merely require that no major objections are presented, that the bot performs a limited test run of edits, and that the bot operator is in good standing in the community.

Despite the means for a community review, often only a handful (or less) of the local editors take part in the process. Indeed, even on some of the larger language versions, there exists only a small developer community operating bots or interested in their approval. From Dutch to Slovenian, bureaucrats report a small number of contributors active in the review process. Finnish Bureaucrat EJS-80 explains: "In practice, the bureaucrat usually gives or denies a bot flag after a test run, and comments from other users than the bureaucrat are relatively rare. If there are comments from other users, they usually point out errors in [the] bot's edits. So, it's generally a process of passive acceptance." On some versions like the Slovenian Wikipedia, a single bureaucrat who watches over the local bot request-for-approvals page generally handles the reviews.

The third, least common bot approval process is one that is managed by a distinct group of contributors invested in the local bot community. The largest and oldest such body is the Bot Approvals Group (BAG) on the English Wikipedia. Established in 2006 to review the soundness of bot requests and determine community consensus around bot tasks, an on-wiki job that one previous member claimed was "a largely ignored and thankless job," the BAG has weathered accusations of being an insular technical cabal and today continues to monitor bots on the English project. Members are nominated (or self-nominated) to join the group, affirming for the community both their programming history and track record on Wikipedia, as well as stating their interest in joining the group. After a week of community discussion, an "uninvolved bureaucrat" makes a decision as to whether consensus was reached around the candidate.[31] The BAG currently has eight active members and thirty-seven semiactive or inactive members.[32] The BAG does not preclude non-BAG members from participating in the review process, and other members of the bot community do participate within this highly structured and chaperoned system.

The Portuguese Wikipedia is a second large language version to use an approvals group process, which was put into place in January 2011. The previous policy allowed a bot operator to appeal directly to a bureaucrat, who usually had little technical knowledge to make educated decisions. Once a bot flag was granted, there was no process for reviewing new bot tasks, so bot operators were at liberty to rework their scripts as they saw fit. Worried by this lack of accountability, User Alchimista proposed that a group be formed to more closely monitor both the granting of the bot flag and the expansion of bots for additional tasks. Like most language versions, there are only a small number of local bot operators on the Portuguese Wikipedia, so only a small approvals group is necessary. Alchimista adapted the English Wikipedia's BAG model for the local project, establishing the Grupo de Aprovação de Bots with members elected by the community; currently four members make up the group.[33] In addition to more thoroughly vetted bots, though, Alchimista credits the new process with establishing something more human on the project as well, a local bot community: "Over the years, a bot only needed to get initial approval, so [when bot operators] got the flag, they didn't need to interact with other people. Now, to perform a task that would change a lot of articles, that task needs approval, so people [are] getting into a more familiar community."

These three bot approval processes—a bureaucrat review, a community review, and an approvals group review—represent a common evolution within Wikipedia over time from unrestricted participation to a more fleshed-out, process-driven contribution model. As local projects grew in size, their technical contributors realized the dangers inherent in one-person bureaucrat reviews, and many bot policies still retain language pointing out the risks and potential disruptions that poorly executed or supervised bots can cause (figure 1.2). The solution for many language versions has been a policy and process that is structured and based on the consensus approvals, and yet open and flexible enough so as not to alienate technical contributors. The additional supervision built into the approvals group approach, epitomized by the BAG on the English-language version, offers bureaucracy purposefully avoided by other versions; as Dutch and Commons User Multichill, an early interwiki bot operator, described: "The bureaucratic culture on English [Wikipedia], which clashes with other cultures . . . actually scared off a lot of bot operators who don't feel like dealing with it." Yet the English-language version, with twice as many total bots and a much larger local bot population than any other version, faces a much larger demand for the time and attention of its technical bot community, and the guidance of the BAG maintains an always active review process.

Far from the early days of "Ignore All Rules," Wikipedia policies, whether simple or complex, are "developed by the community to describe best practices, clarify principles, resolve conflicts, and otherwise further our goal of creating a free, reliable encyclopedia."[34] They are "intended to reflect the consensus of the community,"[35] but it is important not to overlook the incredibly small size of the bot "community" on even the largest language versions; these editors, both because of their expertise and the general lack of interest from the larger Wikipedia community, influence nearly all areas of the project, and their purview over both policy and code, as Lessig reminds us,[36] make them powerful sociotechnical actors.

AN UNCERTAIN FUTURE

Despite the fun that some bot operators have with the user pages of their pro-grammed creations, this small subpopulation of Wikipedia contributors almost universally points to one overarching value of bot work on the site: it frees human editors to work on more content. This value cannot be overlooked, as recent data from the Wikimedia Foundation (WMF) has indicated a plateau and possible de-cline in the project's active contributor base.[37] But while bots are designed to oper-ate unsupervised, and in fact sometimes continue editing on the site even after bot operators have ceased monitoring them—User Cyde, whose Cydebot has made over two million edits on the English Wikipedia, refers to these (including his own) as "zombie bots"[38]—it is a mistake to fetishize these actors in either a literal or Marxian sense, as they are very much the product of social relations and human engineer-ing, or to look to them as an alternative to human contributions. With the WMF's difficulty in attracting new content contributors comes difficulty in attracting new programmers and developers to contribute automated tools as well, especially at a local level. Many large language versions have small developer communities that, as Russian User Rubin16 explained, always need "fresh blood."

The significance of bots for Wikipedia moving forward is also uncertain because of the WMF's first new major project since 2006, Wikidata.[39] Originally concep-tualized as early as 2004,[40] Wikidata officially launched in October 2012 with the purpose of creating "a free knowledge base about the world that can be read and edited by humans and machines alike. It will provide data in all the languages of the Wikimedia projects, and allow for the central access to data in a similar vein as Wikimedia Commons does for multimedia files."[41] The project's impact on interwiki bots will be large, as Wikidata will provide a central repository for interwiki links, allowing all local language versions to import this data and end their reliance on EmausBot, SieBot, and other global bots to carry out these interwiki tasks. Steward Pathoschild speculates that Wikidata may even "make the [Global bot] policy obso-lete by eliminating the need for interwiki bots altogether." The Hungarian Wikipedia was the first to make use of Wikidata's interlanguage links in January 2013,[42] with all other Wikipedias following suit over the following three months.

The era of interwiki bots may be over for Wikipedia, and the significant and sometimes surprising percentage of bot edits to both large and small language versions will certainly be reduced. The bots whose tasks will be displaced by Wikidata will need to be repurposed or retired, their operators forced to deal with the changing technical infrastructure of the project. Actor-network theory tells us this is a black box being opened, a once stable assemblage of heterogeneous actors now forced to make new alliances or leave the network of relations completely. Indeed, ANT directs us to avoid both technological determinism when considering bots and social determinism when considering policies, as each of these are material-semiotic networks of meaning, practice, and substance that shift over time. Wikidata's adoption will create new alliances and new black boxes among Wikipedia's sociotechnical actors, informed both by the historical record of bots and programmers on the site and current pressures of the network to improve and evolve.

Wikipedians in general, and bot operators specifically, are a fiercely pragmatic lot, though, who understand their work in terms of real-world action, not the application of social theory. The newly freed-up capacity and skill of these programmers and contributors could fill what seems a clear void by turning their attention to local-level issues, while at the same time monitoring global developments to the project that may require their expertise.

Wikidata is, by its very definition, a sociotechnical enterprise, a database for both humans and machines to read and write. It is the latest development for a project that's sociotechnical roots stretch back to its founders' adoption of the wiki as the best technological tool to support the aggregation of human knowledge.[43] The global community of contributors that emerged to write the world's largest encyclopedia and to support the goals of democratic and free information quickly validated that decision. Indeed, the shining idea/ideal of Wikipedia is marketed to the masses for its social and cultural possibilities, but behind the scenes, it is sociotechnical collaboration—human intelligence and programmed muscle—that drives much of the site. Bot operators and the work of their creations, often quite simple, yet sometimes remarkably advanced, have a long and rich tradition on Wikipedia, but their story is largely one known only to those in it. Most in this group are fine with this relative anonymity. Of course, this, too, is a convention of the community's own sociotechnical understanding of itself: whether you're a writer, an administrator, a vandalism patroller, a consensus-builder, a janitor,[44] or a programmer, you are an "editor" on Wikipedia . . . bots too.

NOTES

1. "Meatbot," Netlingo.com, accessed March 6, 2013, http://www.netlingo.com/word/meatbot.php.
2. "Wikipedia:Bot policy," Wikipedia, accessed March 6, 2013, http://en.wikipedia.org/wiki/Wikipedia:Bot_policy.

3. "Wikipedia:Bot policy."

4. Sabine Niederer and José van Dijck, "Wisdom of the Crowd or Technicity of Content? Wikipedia as a Sociotechnical System," *New Media & Society* 12, no. 8 (2010); Randall Livingstone, "Network of Knowledge: Wikipedia as a Sociotechnical System of Intelligence," PhD diss., University of Oregon, 2012.

5. Niederer and van Dijck, "Wisdom of the Crowd."

6. Joseph Michael Reagle Jr., *Good Faith Collaboration: The Culture of Wikipedia* (Cambridge: MIT Press, 2010), accessed March 6, 2013, http://reagle.org/joseph/2010/gfc/.

7. "List of Wikipedias." Wikimedia, accessed February 29, 2013, http://meta.wikimedia.org/wiki/List_of_Wikipedias.

8. "Bot," Wikimedia, accessed March 9, 2013, http://meta.wikimedia.org/wiki/Bot.

9. Andrew Leonard, *Bots: The Origin of New Species* (San Francisco: Hardwired, 1997).

10. Leonard, *Bots*.

11. "Wikipedia:Robotar," Wikipedia, accessed March 12, 2013, http://sv.wikipedia.org/wiki/Wikipedia:Robotar.

12. R. Stuart Geiger, "The Lives of Bots," in *Critical Point of View: A Wikipedia Reader*, ed. Geert Lovink and Nathaniel Tkacz (Amsterdam: Institute of Network Cultures, 2011), 78–93.

13. Geiger, "The Lives of Bots," 79.

14. Michel Callon, "The Sociology of an Actor-Network: The Case of the Electric Vehicle," in *Mapping the Dynamics of Science and Technology*, ed. by Michel Callon, John Law, and Arie Rip (New York: Macmillan, 1986), 19–34; Bruno Latour, *Science in Action* (Cambridge: Harvard University Press, 1987).

15. Bruno Latour, "Technology Is Society Made Durable," in *A Sociology of Monsters: Essays on Power, Technology, and Domination*, ed. John Law (London: Routledge, 1991), 103–31.

16. Bruno Latour, *Reassembling the Social: An Introduction to Actor-Network Theory* (Oxford: Oxford University Press, 2005).

17. Lawrence Lessig, *Code: Version 2.0* (New York: Basic Books, 2006); Alexander Galloway, *Protocol: How Control Exists after Decentralization* (Cambridge: MIT Press, 2004).

18. "Wikipedia:Bot policy."

19. "Wikipédia:Bot," Wikipedia, accessed March 16, 2013, http://fr.wikipedia.org/w/index.php?title=Wikip%C3%A9dia:Bot&oldid=75632; "Wikipedia:Bots/Liste der Bots," Wikipedia, accessed March 16, 2013, http://de.wikipedia.org/wiki/Wikipedia:Bots/Liste_der_Bots.

20. Niederer and van Dijck, "Wisdom of the Crowd."

21. Erik Zachte, "Wikipedia Statistics," accessed February 28, 2013, http://stats.wikimedia.org/EN/BotActivityMatrixEdits.htm.

22. Bo Leuf and Ward Cunningham, *The Wiki Way: Quick Collaboration on the Web* (Boston: Addison-Wesley, 2001).

23. "Interwiki bot," Wikimedia, accessed March 10, 2013, http://meta.wikimedia.org/wiki/Interwiki_bot.

24. "Bot policy," Wikimedia, accessed March 10, 2013, http://meta.wikimedia.org/wiki/Bot_policy.

25. "Wiki sets: Global bot wikis," Wikimedia, accessed March 10, 2013, http://meta.wikimedia.org/wiki/Special:WikiSets/2.

26. A Turkic language of the Bashkirs, mainly spoken in the Russian republic of Bashkortostan. See "Bashkir language," Wikipedia, accessed March 10, 2013, http://en.wikipedia.org/wiki/Bashkir_language.

27. Alissa Skelton, "Wikipedia Volunteer Editor Reaches 1 Million Edits," Mashable, accessed March 10, 2013, http://mashable.com/2012/04/23/wikipedia-volunteer-editor/.

28. EmausBot and Luckas-bot were created by Russian User Emaus and Portuguese User Luckas Blade, respectively.

29. "Contributors Wikipedia:Bot_policy," Toolserver, accessed March 12, 2013, http://toolserver.org/~daniel/WikiSense/Contributors.php?wikilang=en&wikifam=.wikipedia.org&grouped=on&page=Wikipedia:Bot_policy.

30. "Wikipèdia:Bot/Statut," Wikipedia, accessed March 12, 2013, http://fr.wikipedia.org/wiki/Wikip%C3%A9dia:Bot/Statut.

31. "Wikipedia:Bot Approvals Group," Wikipedia, accessed March 12, 2013, http://en.wikipedia.org/wiki/Wikipedia:Bot_Approvals_Group.

32. "Wikipedia:Bot Approvals Group."

33. "Wikipédia:Robôs:Grupo de aprovação," Wikipedia, accessed March 12, 2013, http://pt.wikipedia.org/wiki/Wikip%C3%A9dia:Rob%C3%B4s/Grupo_de_aprova%C3%A7%C3%A3o.

34. "Wikipedia:Policies and guidelines," Wikipedia, accessed June 21, 2013, http://en.wikipedia.org/wiki/Wikipedia:Policies_and_guidelines.

35. "Wikipedia:Policies and guidelines."

36. Lessig, *Code: Version 2.0.*

37. Wikimedia Foundation, "Wikimedia Strategic Plan: A Collaborative Vision for the Movement through 2015," accessed March 18, 2013, http://strategy.wikimedia.org/wiki/Main_Page.

38. Ben McIlwain, "The Highest-Editing Zombie Bot on Wikipeda," accessed March 18, 2013, http://www.cydeweys.com/blog/2008/05/26/wikipedia-zombie-bot/.

39. "Wikidata," Wikipedia, accessed March 18, 2013, http://en.wikipedia.org/wiki/Wikidata.

40. "Wikidata/2005 proposal," MediaWiki, accessed March 18, 2013, http://www.mediawiki.org/wiki/Wikidata/2005_proposal.

41. "Wikidata," Wikimedia, accessed March 18, 2013, https://meta.wikimedia.org/wiki/Wikidata.

42. Lydia Pintscher, "First Steps of Wikidata in the Hungarian Wikipedia," Wikimedia Deutschland, accessed March 18, 2013, http://blog.wikimedia.de/2013/01/14/first-steps-of-wikidata-in-the-hungarian-wikipedia/.

43. Andrew Lih, *The Wikipedia Revolution: How a Bunch of Nobodies Created the World's Greatest Encyclopedia* (New York: Hyperion, 2009).

44. Olof Sundin, "Janitors of Knowledge: Constructing Knowledge in the Everyday Life of Wikipedia Editors," *Journal of Documentation* 67, no. 5 (2011): 840–62

2

The Most Controversial Topics in Wikipedia

A Multilingual and Geographical Analysis

Taha Yasseri, Anselm Spoerri, Mark Graham, and János Kertész

INTRODUCTION

Value creation in electronic collaborative environments is rapidly gaining importance. Examples include the Open Source Software project, applications for social network services, and the paradigmatic case of Wikipedia. The latter is especially suited for scientific research as practically all changes and discussions are recorded and made publicly available. This provides a unique opportunity to study the laws of peer production, the process of self-organization of hierarchical structures needed to make such a system efficient, and the occurring regional and cultural differences.

One of the challenges is to understand the emergence and resolution of conflicts in peer production. While the common aim in the collaboration is clear, unavoidably differences in opinions and views occur, leading to controversies. Clearly, there is a positive role of the conflicts: if they can be resolved in a consensus, the resulting product will better reflect the state of the art without fighting conflicts out. However, there are examples, where no hope for a consensus seems in sight—then the struggle strongly limits efficiency. The investigation of conflicts in Wikipedia can contribute not only to the understanding of the mechanisms of peer production but also to the nature of the conflict itself. What are the dynamics of the emergence of a conflict? What are the main elements of the escalation? How are the camps structured? What are the main techniques of reaching consensus? These are all general questions, and there is a large amount of literature about them in political sciences, sociology, and social psychology (see, e.g., Schelling 1980 and Jeong 2008). A major problem in the quantitative analysis of conflicts is the lack of appropriate measures and sufficient amount of data. Wikipedia is a special environment, but its complete documentation makes it particularly suited for such quantitative studies. We hope to gain information not only about conflicts and their resolution under collaborative task-solving

25

circumstances but also about the general nature of controversies. In addition, the presence of different editions of Wikipedia for different languages allows us to investigate all the mentioned research questions on a global scale and cross-lingually, aiming at understanding universal and local features of the conflicts. Cross-cultural comparisons of contested and controversial topics provide us with a detailed and naturally generated image of the priorities and sensitivities of the editors' community of the specific language edition.

Our interest in this study is mainly of a sociopolitical nature. By using and comparing twelve different language editions of Wikipedia, we were interested in cultural differences and similarities, and we investigated whether Wikipedia is a multicultural forum or if there are strong linguistic-group-dependent features. Here we use visualizations to assist us in disentangling this multivariate issue. Our findings suggest that on the one hand Wikipedia as a unifying tool brings divergent groups of individuals closer to each other, but on the other hand there are still specific characteristics to be understood only based on localities and cultural differences. One approach to this issue is to investigate the effects coming from geographical locations of controversial topics in different language editions of Wikipedia. A further approach is to identify and visualize the contested topics that are shared in different languages and cultures as well as show which topics are specific to a language.

There is an increasing body of literature on Wikipedia conflicts; for a recent review see Yasseri and Kertész (2013). The first problem to solve is to create an automated filter to identify controversial articles that work independently of all the languages of Wikipedia. While there are lists of controversial topics and "lamest edit wars" in Wikipedia provided by editor communities, it has been argued that those lists are neither complete nor exclusive (Sumi et al. 2011a). As such, there have been several efforts to introduce quantitative algorithms to detect and rank controversial articles in Wikipedia (Kittur et al. 2007; Vuong et al. 2008; Sumi et al. 2011a, 2011b). Here a compromise between efficiency and accuracy is called for. Among the one-dimensional measures that can be computed, the one developed by Sumi et al. (2011a) turns out to be one of the most reliable ones (Sepehri Rad and Barbosa 2012). Using this measure, detailed studies of the statistics (Sumi et al. 2011b), dynamics, and characteristics of conflicts in different versions of Wikipedia (Yasseri et al. 2012) were carried out. In this work, we use the same methodology to locate and rank the controversial articles and then compare their topical coverage and geographical locations (where possible) across different language editions.

Previous work on topical coverage of contested articles in English Wikipedia (Kittur, Chi, and Suh 2009) has reported that religion and philosophy are among the most debated topics. However, this study doesn't give more detailed information about the individual articles with high levels of controversy or a comparison between different language editions. The detection methods used by Kittur, Chi, and Suh (2009) are based on the "controversial tags" assigned by editors to the articles, which evidently does not include all the debated articles and is hard to generalize to language editions beyond English (Sumi et al. 2011b).

Apic, Betts, and Russell (2011) also took the user-tagged articles in the English Wikipedia into account and calculated a "dispute" index for each country based on the number of tagged articles linking to the article about the country. They show that this index correlates with external measures for governance, political, and economical stability, such that the higher the dispute index the lower the stability: Wikipedia Dispute Index correlates negatively with the World Bank Policy: Research Aggregate Governance Indicator (WGI) for political stability with R = −0.781.

METHODS

In this section, we briefly describe the controversy detection methods and the visualization methods used to present the results.

Controversy Detection Method and Topical Categorization

We quantify the controversiality of an article based on its editorial history by focusing on "reverts"—that is, when an editor undoes another editor's edit completely and returns the Wikipedia article back to its most recent, preedited version. To detect reverts, we first assign a MD5 hash code (Rivest 1992) to each revision of the article, and then by comparing the hash codes we detect when two versions in the history line are exactly the same. In this case, the latest edit (leading to the second identical revision) is marked as a "revert," and a pair of editors, namely a reverting and a reverted one, is recognized. A "mutual revert" is recognized if a pair of editors (x, y) is observed once with x and once with y as the reverter. The weight of an editor x is defined as the number of edits N performed by him or her, and the weight of a mutually reverting pair is defined as the minimum of the weights of the two editors. The controversiality M of an article is defined by summing the weights of all mutually reverting editor pairs, excluding the topmost pair, and multiplying this number by the total number of editors E involved in the article. This results in the following:

$$M = E \sum_{\text{all mutual reverts}} min(N^{\text{d}}, N^{\text{r}})$$

where N r/d is the number of edits for the article committed by the reverting/reverted editor. The sum is taken over mutual reverts rather than single reverts because reverting is very much part of the normal workflow, especially for defending articles from vandalism. The minimum of the two weights is used because conflicts between two senior editors contribute more to controversiality than conflicts between a junior and a senior editor, or between two junior editors. And finally, the topmost reverting pair is excluded to avoid overestimating the editorial war dominated by a personal fight between two single editors. The explained measure can be easily calculated for each article, irrespective of the language, size, and length of its history.

Visualization of Topical Overlaps

The searchCrystal visualization toolset will be used to compare, visualize, and identify Wikipedia pages that are highly contested in multiple languages. Similar to a bull's-eye display, searchCrystal uses a radial mapping so that the Wikipedia pages contained in *all* the language lists that are being compared are mapped to the *center* of the display and the number of lists that contain the same page decreases toward the periphery of the display. SearchCrystal consists of several complementary views: the category, cluster, spiral, and list views (Spoerri 2004a, 2004b, 2004c). Each view helps the user explore specific aspects of the overlap structure between the lists being compared.

Similar to a Venn diagram, the category view provides an aggregated view since it groups all the pages that are contained in the same combination of lists and shows how many pages are included in which specific combinations of languages (see figures 2.2 and 2.6). At its periphery, star-shaped icons with a single color represent the specific lists that are being compared. Each list is assigned a unique color, and the number inside a star-shaped icon indicates the number of pages in the list; the text label next to the star-shaped icon indicates which language (or combination of languages) is used as a crystal input. The interior of the category view consists of circular icons whose colored sectors indicate which specific lists contain the same page. The size of a circular icon indicates how many pages are contained in a specific combination of lists. At the edge of a circular icon, the two pages with the highest list positions are also shown.

The cluster view shows how the *individual* Wikipedia pages are related to the lists being compared, and a radial mapping is used to map pages into concentric rings based on the number of lists that contain them (see figures 2.3, 2.4, and 2.5). In this view, the star-shaped icons at the periphery act like "magnets" that pull a page icon toward them based on the page's list positions (Spoerri 2004a). Thus, the position of a page icon reflects the relative difference between the page's positions in the lists that include it. Further, pages are mapped into the same circular ring if they are contained in the same number of lists. The closer a page is placed toward the display center within a ring, the higher the average of its list positions. A page icon has multiple visual properties to help the user determine how many and which specific lists contain the page and the page's average position in the lists. The shape of a page icon indicates the number of lists that contain the page, and the colors indicate which lists. The size of a page icon reflects the average position of the page in the lists that contain it. The greater the size and the stronger the color saturation of a page icon, the higher up it is placed in the lists. Thus, both the position of a page icon inside its designated ring and its size and color saturation indicate whether a page is highly placed in the lists that include it. The page title is displayed next to a page icon, but it can be truncated to prevent titles from overlapping.

The spiral view places all pages sequentially along an expanding spiral, so that the distance of page icons from the display center is the same as in the cluster view (see figure 2.7). Pages that are included in all of the lists being compared are located in the center ring. The icons for pages that are contained in the same number of lists are placed consecutively along the spiral and in the same concentric ring. Title fragments are displayed in the radial direction to make effective use of the white space in the spiral layout (Spoerri 2004b). The spiral view, which can be rotated, makes it possible for users to rapidly scan a large number of pages and their titles.

Geographic Data

In order to determine the geographic coordinates of Wikipedia articles, we drew upon the efforts of the Oxford Internet Institute's geographic article parser (see Graham 2011 or https://github.com/oxfordinternetinstitute/wikiproject). The data were all taken from 2012 Wikipedia data dumps, and we searched for coordinates in every article. If an article had a coordinate in any language edition, we assigned that same coordinate to the equivalent articles in all other languages. We improved the quality of our coordinates by doing things like eliminating or fixing erroneous coordinates and making sure to remove irrelevant coordinates (Wikipedia actually contains a lot of coordinates for extraterrestrial entities such as lunar craters![1]). We also excluded articles that are essentially indexes of places from our geographic data set as they tell us little about any particular parts of the world (e.g., articles about events, monuments, towns, etc.). We thus reduced the data set to all articles with four or fewer sets of coordinates and used the coordinates that appear most frequently (if all coordinates appeared once, we used the first set).

RESULTS

We have calculated the controversiality M for all the articles available in ten different language editions of Wikipedia based on the data dumps we downloaded in March 2010. We tried to gather as diverse a sample as possible including West European, East European, and Middle Eastern languages within the language capabilities of our research team. The selected language editions span a wide range in terms of the number of articles (and active editors): English, German, French, with more than 1 million articles (and 19, 1.7, and 1.6 million editors, respectively); Spanish, with more than 500,000 articles (2.7 million editors); Persian, Czech, Hungarian, Arabic, and Romanian with more than 200,000 (with 350,000, 230,000, 235,000, 645,000, and 264,000 editors, respectively); and finally Hebrew with 142,000 articles and 200,000 editors. The more than 27 million editors and potential readers of these language editions have a much extended geographical distribution, and that enables us to investigate the disputed titles and topics at the global scale.

Different selections of the lists of M scores are available at http://wwm.phy.bme .hu/ to download. In table 2.1, the top ten lists of the most controversial articles with the highest M's are provided. By looking at the titles, already a rough impression on the topical coverage of the editorial wars in each language can be gained. For example, *Jesus* appears among the top ten in English, German, French, and Czech Wikipedias. Religion, politics, and geographical places seem to be the common fields of editorial wars in all editions; however, it is with local effects: far-right politics and nationalism in Hungarian, current Iranian political figures in Persian, sex- and gender-related topics in Czech, and football clubs in Spanish Wikipedias are evident examples for these localities. To be able to compare the disputed articles at the title level, we needed to "transform" all the topics to English. To this end, we have used the Wikipedia interlanguage links created and modified by editors and automated robots. We replaced all the titles by the corresponding title in the English Wikipedia. However, in a few cases, there was no article about exactly the same topic in English Wikipedia, and so we kept the original title. In figure 2.1, a word cloud of all the one thousand titles generated by this process is depicted. The size of the words is proportional to their appearance frequency. The cloud is self-explanatory, and it already shows some common patterns among the most controversial topics.

We demonstrate and analyze these overlaps at the level of article titles in the next section.

Overlapping Lists and the Patterns

The searchCrystal visualization toolset is used to first visualize the overlap between these language groupings: 1) English, German, French, Spanish; 2) Czech, Hungarian, Romanian; and 3) Arabic, Persian, Hebrew. Next, the overlap between these language groupings is visualized to identify Wikipedia pages that are highly contested in multiple language sets. An interactive version of searchCrystal can be accessed at http://comminfo.rutgers.edu/~aspoerri/searchCrystal/searchCrystal_editWars_ALL. html, and a screencast provides a quick overview on how the visualizations were created at http://comminfo.rutgers.edu/~aspoerri/searchCrystal/WikiEditWars _Screencast/WikiEditWars_Screencast.html.

In figure 2.2, the category view is used to show an aggregated view of the overlap structure between the most contested Wikipedia pages in English, German, French, and Spanish: the two pages about *homeopathy* and *Jesus*, respectively, are contested in all four languages; five pages are contested in three out of the four languages, and, for example, *global warming* and *socialism* are contested pages in the English-, German-, and French-language versions of Wikipedia; thirty-four pages are contested in two out of four languages. Examining the icons that represent the pages that are contested in only one of the four languages, sixty-seven of the one hundred most contested pages in English are not contested in the other three languages. English

Table 2.1. Top Ten Most Controversial Articles in Each Language Edition of Wikipedia. (Titles in italic are literally translated; the rest are the titles of the sister articles in English Wikipedia.)

en	De	Ro	fr	es	cs
George W. Bush	Croatia	FC Universitatea Craiova	Ségolène Royal	Chile	Homosexuality
Anarchism	Scientology	Mircea Badea	Unidentified flying object	Club América	Psychotronics
Muhammad	9/11 conspiracy theories	Disney Channel (Romania)	Jehovah's Witnesses	Opus Dei	Telepathy
LWWE[1]	*Fraternities*	Legionnaires' rebellion and Bucharest pogrom	Jesus	Athletic Bilbao	Communism
Global warming	Homeopathy	Lugoj	Sigmund Freud	Andrés Manuel López Obrador	Homophobia
Circumcision	Adolf Hitler	Vladimir Tismăneanu	September 11 attacks	Newell's Old Boys	Jesus
United States	Jesus	Craiova	Muhammad al-Durrah incident	FC Barcelona	Moravia
Jesus	Hugo Chávez	Romania	Islamophobia	Homeopathy	Sexual orientation change efforts
Race and intelligence	Minimum wage	Traian Băsescu	God in Christianity	Augusto Pinochet	Ross Hedvíček
Christianity	Rudolf Steiner	Romanian Orthodox Church	Nuclear power debate	Alianza Lima	Israel

hu	ar	fa	he
Gypsy crime	Ash'ari	Báb	Chabad
Atheism	*Ali bin Talal al Jahani*	Fatmah	Chabad messianism
Hungarian radical right	Muhammad	Mahmoud Ahmadinejad	2006 Lebanon War
Viktor Orbán	Ali	People's Mujahedin of Iran	B'Tselem
Hungarian Guard Movement	Egypt	Criticism of the Quran	Benjamin Netanyahu
Ferenc Gyurcsány's speech in May 2006	Syria	Tabriz	*Jewish settlement in Hebron*
The Mortimer case	Sunni Islam	Ali Khamenei	Daphni Leef
Hungarian far right	Wahhabi	Ruhollah Khomeini	Gaza War
Jobbik	Yasser al-Habib	Massoud Rajavi	Beitar Jerusalem F.C.
Polgár Tamás	Arab people	Muhammad	Ariel Sharon

1 List of World Wrestling Entertainment, Inc., employees,ww
en: English; de: German; fr: French; es: Spanish; cs: Czech; hu: Hungarian; ro: Romanian; ar: Arabic; fa: Persian; he: Hebrew

Figure 2.1. Word cloud made of the titles of one thousand of the most controversial articles in the ten language editions under study.

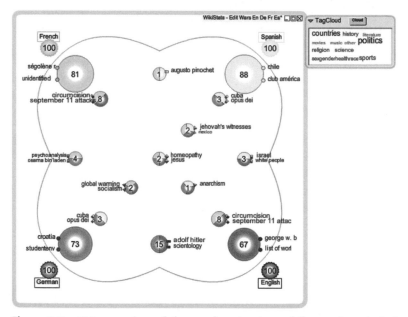

Figure 2.2. Category view of the overlap structure of the most contested Wikipedia pages in English, German, French, and Spanish.

has the most pages (33 percent) that are also contested in one or more of the other languages, whereas Spanish has the fewest pages (12 percent) that are also contested in another language.

In figure 2.3, the cluster view is used to visualize the overlap between the most contested pages in English, German, French, and Spanish, and it uses a *fish-eye transformation* to visually emphasize the pages that are contested in at least two languages (Spoerri 2004c). The *homeopathy* and *Jesus* pages are contested in all the four languages, and their diamond-shaped icons are placed close to the display center, which indicates that they are on average highly contested in all the four languages. The Details-on-Demand display shown below the TagCloud panel in the top right corner shows that the *Jesus* page is one of the top ten contested pages for English, German, and French and the forty-second most contested page for Spanish. For the pages that are contested in three of the four languages, the *Jehovah's Witnesses* page is relatively highly contested in English, French, and Spanish, as is the *anarchism* page in English, German, and Spanish, and their respective triangular icons are placed close to the display center. The *global warming* and *socialism* pages are not as highly contested in English, German, and French, and their respective triangular icons are placed close to the middle of the ring that contains pages that are contested in three

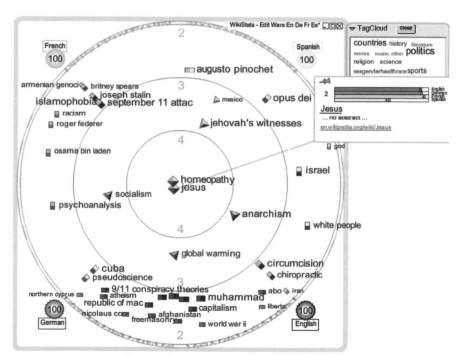

Figure 2.3. Cluster view of the overlap structure of the most contested Wikipedia pages in English, German, French, and Spanish.

of the four languages. The *Mexico* page is moderately contested in English, French, and Spanish, and thus its triangular icon has a smaller size, less saturated colors, and is placed further away from the display center than the other pages that are contested in three of the four languages.

In figure 2.4, the cluster view is used to visualize the overlap between the most contested pages in Czech, Hungarian, and Romanian, and it also uses a fish-eye transformation to visually emphasize the pages that are contested in at least two languages. Specifically, it shows that the Wikipedia page about *Google* is contested in Czech, Hungarian, and Romanian, but its triangular icon is placed away from the center, and this indicates that this page is not one of the most contested pages in the respective languages. Further, five pages are contested in at least two of the three languages: *The Holocaust* and *Romani people* pages are highly contested in both Hungarian and Romanian since their icons are placed closer toward the center; the *Jesus* page is contested in Czech and Romanian, but more so in the Czech Wikipedia since its icon is placed closer to the star-shaped icon that represents the Czech input list of most contested pages.

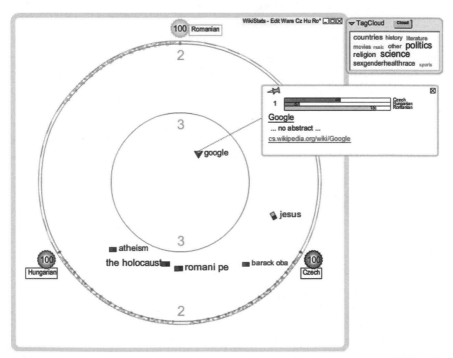

Figure 2.4. Cluster view of the overlap structure of the most contested Wikipedia pages in Czech, Hungarian, and Romanian.

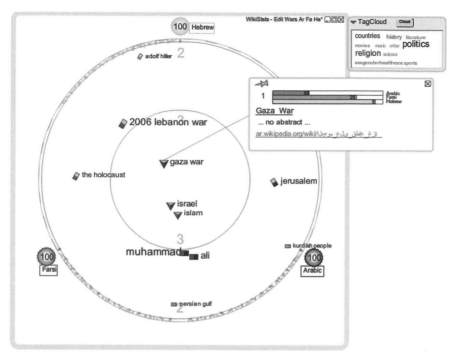

Figure 2.5. Cluster view of the overlap structure of the most contested Wikipedia pages in Arabic, Persian, and Hebrew.

In figure 2.5, the cluster view visualizes the overlap between the most contested pages in Arabic, Persian, and Hebrew, and it also uses a fish-eye transformation to visually emphasize the pages that are contested in at least two languages. Three pages are contested in all three languages, and the *Gaza War* page is the most contested page. Its triangular icon is placed quite close to the display center, which indicates that this page is quite highly contested overall, and since its icon is placed closer to the Hebrew and Persian (Farsi) star-shaped input icons and further away from the Arabic input icon, this indicates that the *Gaza War* page is most contested in Hebrew, a little less so in Persian, and less so in Arabic. The small Details-on-Demand display below the TagCloud shows the list of positions of the *Gaza War* page in the respective languages, where the longer the colored line the higher up in the list the page is placed.

Altogether, eight pages are contested in two of the Arabic-, Persian-, and Hebrew-language versions of Wikipedia: the *Muhammad* page is very highly contested in both Arabic and Persian; the *2006 Lebanon War* page is highly contested in both Hebrew and Persian. Located in the top right corner of the overlap display, a TagCloud panel shows the relative frequency of the categorical topics that are most contested for Arabic, Persian, and Hebrew—*political* and *religious* topics represent the two most contested topics.

As a next step in the visual analysis of the most contested pages in the different language versions of Wikipedia, the unique pages contained in the three language sets can be compared with each other. SearchCrystal makes it possible to use drag and drop operations—see the screencast for a demonstration of how this can be done—to compute the overlap structure between the set of English, German, French, and Spanish pages (350 unique pages); the set of Czech, Hungarian, and Romanian pages (293 unique pages); and the set of Arabic, Persian, and Hebrew pages (286 unique pages), as shown using the category view in figure 2.6. There are seven pages that are contested in all three language sets, the *Israel* and *Adolf Hitler* pages being the most highly contested pages that are contained in all three language sets. Forty-one pages are contested in two of the three language sets, the *Jesus* and *Jehovah's Witnesses* pages being the most highly contested pages that are both contained in the English-, German-, French-, and Spanish-language set and the Czech-, Hungarian-, and Romanian-language set.

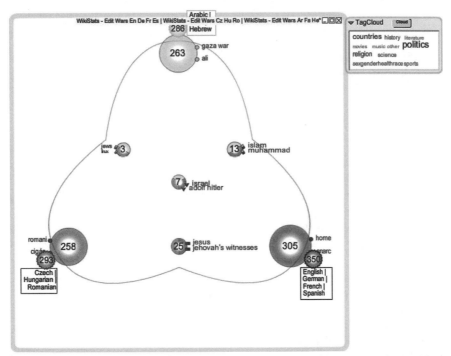

Figure 2.6. Category view of the overlap structure of the most contested Wikipedia pages in the three sets of languages (blue = English, German, French, Spanish; red = Czech, Hungarian, Romanian; green = Arabic, Persian, Hebrew).

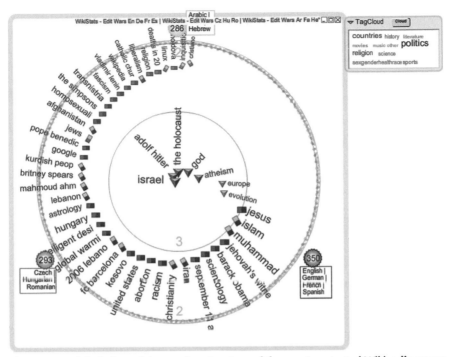

Figure 2.7.   Spiral view of the overlap structure of the most contested Wikipedia pages in the three sets of languages (blue = English, German, French, Spanish; red = Czech, Hungarian, Romanian; green = Arabic, Persian, Hebrew).

As shown in the star-shaped input icons, there are 350 unique English, German, French, and Spanish pages; 293 unique Czech, Hungarian, and Romanian pages; and 286 unique Arabic, Persian, and Hebrew pages.

The *Islam* and *Muhammad* pages are the most highly contested pages that are both contained in the English-, German-, French-, and Spanish-language set and the Arabic-, Persian-, and Hebrew-language set. Roughly 10 percent of the pages in each language set are also contested in another language set. The TagCloud panel shows that pages related to *political* topics represent the largest group of contested pages in the union of all three language sets, followed by pages related to *geographical/countries* and *religious* topics, respectively.

In figure 2.7, the spiral view visualizes the overlap structure of the individual pages contained in the set of English, German, French, and Spanish pages; the set of Czech, Hungarian, and Romanian; and the set of Arabic, Persian, and Hebrew pages.

A fish-eye transformation is used to visually emphasize the pages that are contained in at least two language sets. As described in more detail previously, the closer a page icon is placed toward the display center within a ring, the higher the average of its list positions; the greater the size and the stronger the color saturation of a page icon, the higher up it is placed in the lists. The spiral view can be rotated so that the titles can be read more easily, and so the angle of an icon with respect to the display center does not encode the relative difference between the list positions in the sets being compared, as is the case in the cluster view. The spiral view is designed to make it easy to see the ranking of the pages in terms of their average list positions and the number of language sets that contain them as well as to ascertain whether the pages contained in more than one language set are highly contested pages are not. The *Israel, Adolf Hitler, Holocaust, God, atheism, Europe,* and *evolution* pages are contained in all three language sets, and the pages *Israel, Adolf Hitler, Holocaust,* and *God* are highly contested in all the language sets since their triangular icons are placed close to the center of the display and their sizes and color saturations are close to the highest possible values. The *Jesus, Islam,* and *Muhammad* pages are very highly contested in two of three language sets since their icons are placed closest toward the display center within the ring that contains pages that are contained in two of the language sets.

Topical Coverage of Conflict

While comparing the titles to locate the overlaps, one realizes that there are many articles with slight differences in the title but very similar content in two or more language editions. Our visualization method is not capable of capturing these similarities. Therefore, we have categorized all the articles in top one hundred lists into ten categories based on their primary categorical tags in Wikipedia and also human judgments about their contents.[2] The ten categories and the topics included in each of them are described in table 2.2. Although at the first glance, these ten categories might look insufficient to cover all the one thousand categorized articles

Table 2.2.   The Topical Categories for the Controversial Articles

Category	Topics	Name	%
A	Politics, Politicians, Political Parties, Political Movements and Ideologies	Politics	25
B	Geographical Locations, Countries, Cities, Towns	Countries	17
C	Religion, Cults, Beliefs	Religion	15
D	History, Historical Figures	History	9
E	Sex and Gender, Health, Human Rights, Environment, Social Activism	Sex, Gender, Health, Race	7
F	Science, Technology, Internet, Web	Science	7
G	Sport Clubs, Sport People, Sport Events	Sports	6
H	Literature, Journals, Journalists, Authors, Newspapers, Languages	Literature	4
I	Movies, TV Channels, TV Series, Theaters, Actor, Directors, Animations	Movies	4
J	Songs, Singers, Music Genres, Music Events	Music	3

(one hundred most controversial articles in ten languages), interestingly, there have been only twenty-six articles out of one thousand that did not match any of these ten categories. This indicates a high level of similarity in different language lists at the topical level.

The aggregated populations of the categories for all the one thousand articles are depicted in figure 2.8. Politics-related articles exceed one-quarter of the whole population, and in addition *geographical places* and *religion* cover more than half of the most controversial articles. Arts-related articles including literature, authors, printed and public media, movies and animations, and the entertainment and music industry ranked eight to ten according to the relative population. However, putting all these categories together, it goes beyond 10 percent of the sample.

Although this pattern is universally the same in all language editions to a good extent, there are also interesting local deviations from the overall norm in each edition. In figure 2.9, populations of the topical categories are shown for each language edition. The predominant examples of anomalies are 1) sports in Spanish Wikipedia, 2) religion, geography, and history in Arabic, Persian, and Hebrew, 3) science- and technology related topics in French and Czech, and finally 4) the arts in the Romanian Wikipedia. It is clearly due to cultural differences and the variation of community priorities from one language to others.

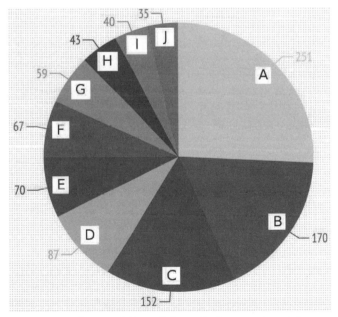

Figure 2.8. The population of the topical categories of the one thousand most controversial articles in ten different language editions. Categories are described in table 2.2.

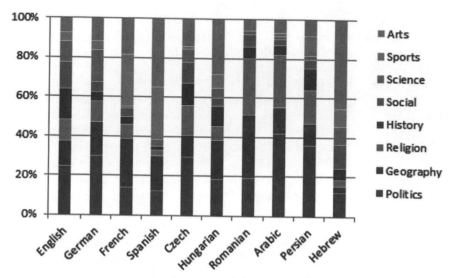

Figure 2.9. Category population separated for each language edition, showing the deviations from the universal topical patterns.

Geographical Distribution of Conflict

As mentioned earlier, articles on geographical places, countries, cities, towns, and more are among the most populated conflict categories. Moreover, many of articles that are not directly about places are "geotagged" and therefore linked to a geographical location. It could be enormously helpful to make geographical maps of the controversial articles based on their geotags.

When mapping the geographic dispersion of conflict, we see an interesting amount of difference between the different language versions of Wikipedia. Some of the smaller language Wikipedias have a high degree of self-focus in their articles and are characterized by the greatest degree of conflict (see also the work of Hecht and Gergle 2009 for another illustration of how different language communities on Wikipedia tend to write about places close to home). For instance, note the geographic focus of conflict in the Czech and Hebrew Wikipedias in figures 2.10 and 2.11 (with the top five locations of conflict labeled on both maps).

Even when looking at large languages that are primarily spoken in more than one country, we are able to see that a significant amount of self-focus occurs (as can be seen in the maps of conflict in Arabic and Spanish in figures 2.12 and 2.13). However, interestingly, the Middle East often seems to be the exception to this rule. The Spanish and Czech, as well as all languages in our sample (apart from Hungarian and Romanian), include articles in Israel as some of those characterized by the greatest amount of conflict.

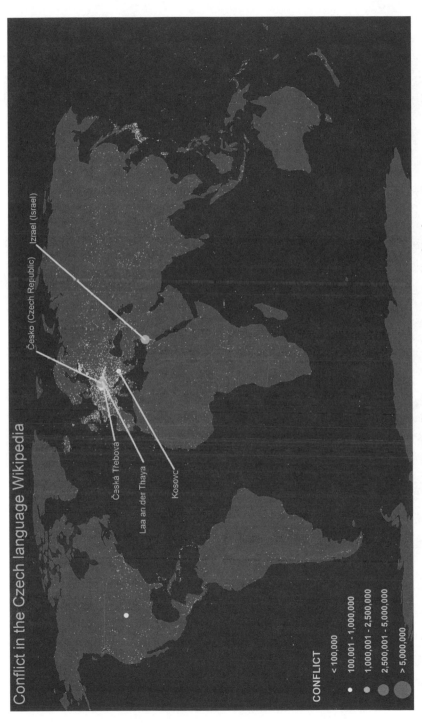

Figure 2.10. Map of conflict in Czech edition of Wikipedia. Size of the dots is proportional to the controversy measure *M*.

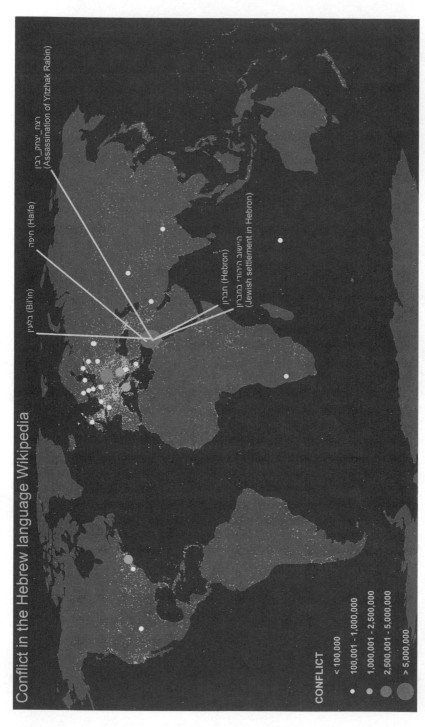

Figure 2.11. Map of conflict in Hebrew edition of Wikipedia. Size of the dots is proportional to the controversy measure *M*.

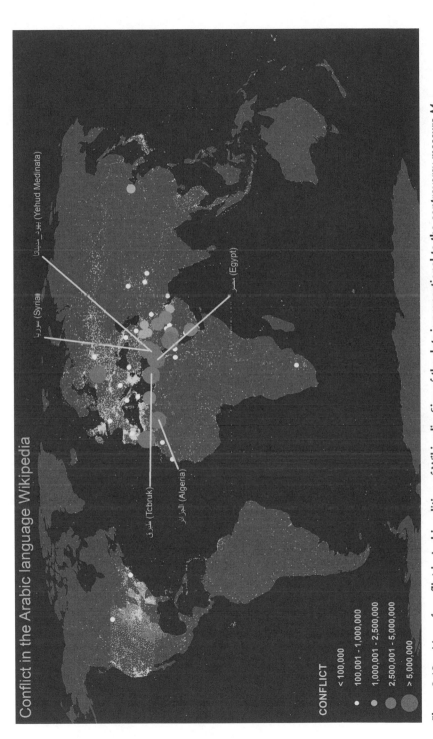

Figure 2.12. Map of conflict in Arabic edition of Wikipedia. Size of the dots is proportional to the controversy measure *M*.

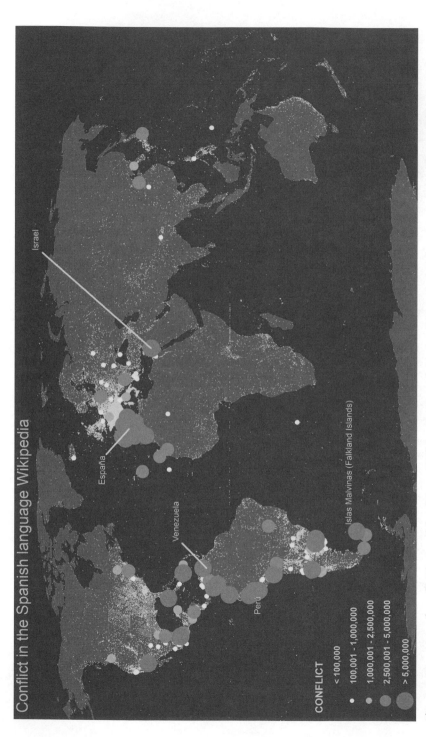

Figure 2.13. Map of conflict in Spanish edition of Wikipedia. Size of the dots is proportional to the controversy measure *M*.

Also worth noting is the fact that we see differences in the geographic topics that generate the most conflict. The articles in Japanese that generate the most conflict are not only all located in Japan but also all educational institutions. The Portuguese articles that generate the most conflict are similarly all located in Brazil (the world's largest Portuguese-speaking nation), with four out of the top five conflict scores being about football teams. (Japanese and Brazilian articles not shown here.)

Within our sample, we actually only see the English, German, and French (shown in figure 2.14) Wikipedias with a significant amount of diversity in the topics and patterns of conflict in geographic articles, indicating a less significant role that specific editors and arguments play in these larger encyclopedias. More maps of different language editions are available at http://www.zerogeography.net/2013/05/mapping-controversy-in-wikipedia.html.

CONCLUSION

In this chapter we have focused on two aspects of the conflict that occurs in different language versions of Wikipedia. First, we explored the overlaps between the most contested articles in different languages. Second, we mapped out the geographical localities of the controversial articles based on their content.

The comparison of the contested articles in multiple languages has demonstrated that there are controversial topics present in several regions and in Wikipedias in many different languages. In particular, the different languages are grouped into three sets: 1) English, German, French, Spanish; 2) Czech, Hungarian, Romanian; and 3) Arabic, Persian, Hebrew. The articles *Israel, Adolf Hitler, Holocaust,* and *God* are highly contested in all of the three language sets, and the *Jesus, Islam,* and *Muhammad* articles are very highly contested in two of three sets of languages. Major religions and religious figures as well as articles related to anti-Semitism and Israel are highly contested in multiple languages and cultures. The controversial articles that occur on a regional scale form a somewhat larger category, like those related to Eastern European history or local conflicts. However, somewhat surprisingly, most of the contested and controversial topics are language dependent.

The English Wikipedia, in particular, occupies a unique role. The language's status as a lingua franca means that English Wikipedia ends up being edited by a broad community beyond those that simply have the language as a "mother tongue" (Yasseri, Sumi, and Kertész 2012). As a result, it is expected that globally disputed themes are often represented in this Wikipedia. Already in the top ten list of conflict articles we see such items as *Jesus, anarchism,* or *race and intelligence.*

Within our sample, we actually only see that the English, German, and French Wikipedias have a significant amount of diversity in the topics and patterns of conflict in geographic articles. This probably indicates the less significant role that specific editors and arguments play in these larger encyclopedias.

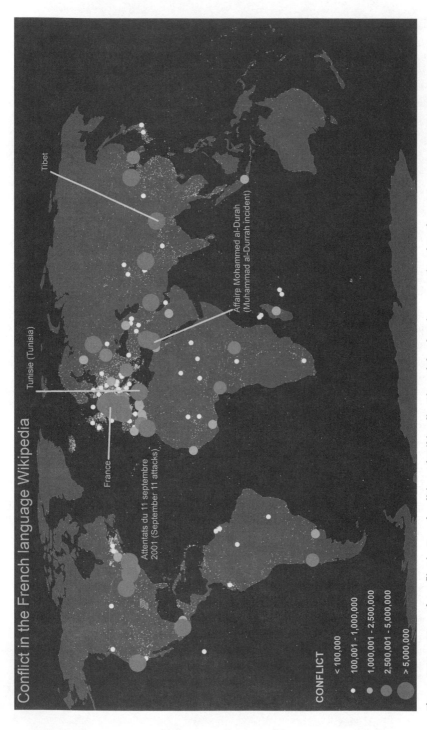

Figure 2.14. Map of conflict in French edition of Wikipedia. Size of the dots is proportional to the controversy measure *M*.

Ultimately by visualizing the controversy in Wikipedia, we are able to see both topics that appear to have crosslinguistic resonance (e.g. Arab-Israeli conflict), and those of a more narrow interest such as the Islas Malvinas/Falkland Islands article in the Spanish Wikipedia. The data presented here therefore offers a window into not just the topics and places that different language communities are interested in, but also the topics that seem worth fighting about.

This visualization-supported research focused on a static picture as obtained from the statistics of conflict articles in different Wikipedias. The controversiality measure M is, however, a dynamic quantity; it allows us to follow the temporal evolution of conflicts (Yasseri et al. 2012; Török et al. 2013). It therefore remains a future task to combine the techniques used here with the study of those dynamic aspects. Furthermore, we see that this work could offer a useful base for more grounded qualitative and critical inquiry into the variable patterns of interest and controversy among different groups in the world's largest encyclopedia.

ACKNOWLEDGMENT

We thank Robert Sumi, András Kornai, András Rung, and Hoda Sepehri Rad for discussions and computational support.

Maps are created based on a data set of geolocated Wikipedia articles prepared by Mark Graham, Bernie Hogan, and Ahmed Medhat.

NOTES

1. Bailly (crater), http://en.wikipedia.org/wiki/Bailly_%28crater%29.
2. Each article is coded by two coders with interceder reliability of 95 to 100 percent for different languages. In cases of mismatching categories, the decision of the more confident coder (native speaker) has been adopted.

REFERENCES

Apic, Gordana, Matthew J. Betts, and Robert B. Russell. 2011. "Content Disputes in Wikipedia Reflect Geopolitical Instability." *PLoS ONE* 6, no. 6: e20902.
Graham, Mark. 2011. "Wiki Space: Palimpsests and the Politics of Exclusion." In *Critical Point of View: A Wikipedia Reader*, edited by Geert Lovink and Nathaniel Tkacz, 269–82. Amsterdam: Institute of Network Cultures.
Hecht, Brent, and Darren Gergle. 2009. "Measuring Self-Focus Bias in Community-Maintained Knowledge Repositories." In *Proceedings of the International Conference on Communities and Technologies (C&T 2009)*. New York: ACM Press, 11–19.
Jeong, Ho-Won. 2008. *Understanding Conflict and Conflict Analysis*. Thousand Oaks, CA: Sage Publications.

Kittur, Aniket, Ed H. Chi, and Bongwon Suh. 2009. "What's in Wikipedia? Mapping Topics and Conflict Using Socially Annotated Category Structure." In *Proceedings of the SIGCHI Conference on Human Factors in Computing Systems (CHI '09)*. New York: ACM, 1509–12.

Kittur, Aniket, Bongwon Suh, Bryan A. Pendleton, and Ed H. Chi. 2007. "He Says, She Says: Conflict and Coordination in Wikipedia." In *CHI 2007*. San Jose, CA: ACM, 453–62.

Rivest, Ronald L. 1992. "The MD5 Message-Digest Algorithm." Internet Request for Comments. RFC, 1321.

Schelling, T. C. 1980. *The Strategy of Conflict*. Cambridge, MA: Harvard University Press.

Sepehri Rad, Hoda, and Denilson Barbosa. 2012. "Identifying Controversial Articles in Wikipedia: A Comparative Study." In *Proceedings of the 8th International Symposium on Wikis and Open Collaboration, WikiSym '12*. Linz, Austria.

Spoerri, Anselm. 2004a. "Visual Editor for Composing Meta Searches." *Proceedings of the 67th Annual Meeting of the American Society for Information Science and Technology (ASIST 2004)* 41, no. 1: 373–82.

———. 2004b. "RankSpiral: Toward Enhancing Search Result Visualizations." In *Proceedings IEEE Information Visualization Symposium (InfoVis 2004)*, 18.

———. 2004c. "Coordinated Views and Tight Coupling to Support Meta Searching." In *Proceedings of the 2nd International Conference on Coordinated & Multiple Views in Exploratory Visualization (CMV 2004)*, 39–48.

———. 2007a. "Visualizing the Overlap between the 100 Most Visited Pages on Wikipedia for September 2006 to January 2007." *First Monday* 12, no. 4.

———. 2007b. "What Is Popular on Wikipedia and Why?" *First Monday* 12, no. 4.

Sumi, Robert, Taha Yasseri, András Rung, András Kornai, and János Kertész. 2011a. "Characterization and Prediction of Wikipedia Edit Wars." In *Proceedings of the ACM WebSci '11*. Koblenz, Germany.

———. 2011b. "Edit Wars in Wikipedia." Paper presented at IEEE Third International Conference on Social Computing (SocialCom), Boston, MA, 724–27.

Török, János, Gerardo Iñiguez, Taha Yasseri, Maxi San Miguel, Kimmo Kaski, and János Kertész. 2013. "Opinions, Conflicts and Consensus: Modeling Social Dynamics in a Collaborative Environment." *Physical Review Letters* 110: 088701.

Vuong, Ba-Quy, Ee-Peng Lim, Aixin Sun, Minh-Tam Le, Hady Wirawan Lauw, and Kuiyu Chang. 2008. "On Ranking Controversies in Wikipedia: Models and Evaluation." In *Proceedings of the 2008 International Conference on Web Search and Data Mining (WSDM '08)*. New York: ACM, 171–82.

Yasseri, Taha, and János Kertész, 2013. "Value Production in a Collaborative Environment." *Journal of Statistical Physics* 151, no. 3–4: 414–39.

Yasseri, Taha, Robert Sumi, and János Kertész. 2012. "Circadian Patterns of Wikipedia Editorial Activity: A Demographic Study." *PloS ONE* 7, no. 1: e30091.

Yasseri, Taha, Robert Sumi, András Rung, András Kornai, and János Kertész. 2012. "Dynamics of Conflicts in Wikipedia." *PLoS ONE* 7, no. 6: e38869.

3

Our News, Their Events?

A Comparison of Archived Current Events on English and Greek Wikipedias

Jahna Otterbacher

INTRODUCTION

Although Wikipedia has its roots in the United States, it has long become a global project. To date, there are Wikipedias in 285 languages, written and maintained by over thirty-nine million registered users around the world.[1] In fact, over 77 percent of Wikipedia articles are written in languages other than English.[2] Despite this diversity, Hara, Shachaf, and Hew (2010) note that most research to date focuses on the English edition. Given the popularity and influence of Wikipedia, it is important to understand its global nature.

Callahan and Herring (2011, 1914) claim that growth trends position English Wikipedia as a "general repository of global knowledge." In contrast, they describe the smaller Wikipedias as having a regional character, emphasizing local values. Like Hara, Shachaf, and Hew (2010), Callahan and Herring call for further cross-cultural research, and they provide specific motivations as explained below.

First, we need a better understanding of the roles of smaller versus larger Wikipedias, and the synergies that could be promoted between them. For instance, given that Wikipedia aims to document and share the world's knowledge, machine translation tools could be used to provide users with access to all available information, no matter which language(s) they read (Callahan and Herring 2011, 1902). However, researchers do not agree as to if and how this should be done, with many arguing that the Wikipedias of smaller languages serve unique needs and audiences (e.g., Jones 2009) such that translated content would be unnecessary and/or undesirable.

In addition, it is necessary to consider the consequences that the global nature of Wikipedia may have for one of its core tenets—the Neutral Point of View (NPOV) Policy. NPOV holds that contributors must present knowledge fairly, "proportionately, and as far as possible without bias,"[3] and has been compared to standards for

Table 3.1. Descriptive Statistics for the English and Greek Wikipedias (as of July 2013)

Language	Rank by Size	Articles	Users	Article per population	Edits/article	Users/ admins
English	1	4,278,837	19,281,986	0.222	145.75	13,390
Greek	49	89,936	128,599	0.699	47.85	6,123

professional journalism (Lih 2004). Yet it seems probable that contributors' cultural backgrounds and languages influence the manner in which they view the world and thus, how they document their knowledge (Kolbitsch and Maurer 2006).

We contribute to the research on the global nature of Wikipedia by examining the archived *current events portal* of the English[4] and the Greek[5] Wikipedias. Like Callahan and Herring (2011), we aim to closely examine the relationship between a regional Wikipedia and the English "global repository." In addition to language and culture, these two communities differ substantially with respect to the size of their repositories and user bases, as shown in table 3.1. While the English Wikipedia is the largest, the Greek Wikipedia currently ranks forty-ninth in size.[6] As will be explained, the current events archived by participants over the past six years will be compared across the two Wikipedias.

ARCHIVING EVENTS OVER TIME: WHAT IS REMEMBERED?

Wikipedia's current events portal is a space where participants collaboratively compile a record of the most important news events on a day-to-day basis. The English guidelines specify that users should log items of international interest, providing a description in complete sentences as well as the "most relevant linked article."[7] Likewise, the Greek-language community's Talk page documents a conversation between users expressing similar goals and norms.[8] Specifically, only significant events should be recorded. ("This page is for recording events of encyclopedic interest . . . not for general news.") In addition, logged events should be documented with "reliable sources close to the events, e.g., news agencies rather than redistributors of news." Each Wikipedia's current events portal is archived regularly, keeping a record of prominent news stories across time.

Scholars have described Wikipedia as a *collective memory place* (e.g., Ferron and Massa 2012; Pentzold 2009), since it provides a space where people across the globe negotiate and make sense of the world. The current events portal is a place where people collectively decide which events in history are memorable enough to be chronicled and, of course, how they should be represented. As our individual memories fade over time, this provides a record of what happened on the international scene during a particular year. There are many questions surrounding the extent to which records differ between Wikipedias. Do Greek- and English-speaking Wikipedians produce different memories of events? Are certain types of news more likely to be recorded by one community versus the other? How are these events represented? Are there methods that enable us to explore such issues on a large scale?

On the one hand, it is likely that cross-culturally, judgments of what constitutes a newsworthy event will vary. For instance, an event closer to home, or happening in a place culturally or historically close to one's home, might be judged as being more important than events happening elsewhere in the world. On the other hand, the biggest stories in the news worldwide tend to feature the same powerful nations, such that Wikipedians at both communities might be exposed to, and in turn log, similar records of events. The current study will use an empirical approach in order to shed light on the questions posed above.

RELATED RESEARCH

In this section, we review the previous work that is most relevant to our study. With the findings in mind, we then focus on specific research questions concerning the current events portal.

Cultural Differences at Wikipedia

In comparative studies across Wikipedias, researchers have studied the *processes* through which users collaboratively create content, as well as characteristics of the *content* itself. To date, this body of work indicates that there are often salient cultural differences across Wikipedias, both in terms of collaborative processes and content.

In an early study, Pfeil, Zaphiris, and Ang (2006) examined the editing patterns behind the article "Game" at four Wikipedias (Dutch, French, German, and Japanese). Their goal was to understand if culture could predict differences in editing patterns among the four communities. Using Hofstede's (1991) dimensions of culture, they found significant correlations between cultural attributes and the likelihood of undertaking a particular task. For instance, they found that the French, who have a high Power Distance Index, are less likely to delete the work of others as compared to Germans, who have a low Power Distance Index. Similarly, Hara, Shachaf, and Hew (2010) relied on Hofstede's framework for studying the connection between culture and collaborative behaviors, examining Talk pages across the English, Hebrew, Japanese, and Malay Wikipedias. A significant finding was that the Eastern cultures, which have a higher power distance, were more likely to make use of politeness tactics (e.g., apologies, greetings) as compared to contributors at the Western Wikipedias. In summary, these studies show that despite sharing a common platform, Wikipedians around the globe do not collaborate and communicate with one another in a uniform manner. These findings resonate with those in the information systems literature that document a strong connection between a collaborative system's uses and ultimate outcome, and the national culture of a group adopting it (Leidner and Kayworth 2006).

Claims that there are important *content differences* across Wikipedias have been expressed for several years (e.g., Kolbitsch and Maurer 2006), and researchers have begun exploring this empirically. Hecht and Gergle (2010) provided convincing evidence that the knowledge contributed to Wikipedia is not consistent cross-culturally. In their study of twenty-five Wikipedias, they found that the majority of articles (74 percent) appeared in only one Wikipedia. Likewise, almost all articles (95 percent) were common across seven or fewer versions. Even within English Wikipedia, topical coverage varies according to the interest of users, and certain topics receive more attention than others (Halavais and Lackaff 2008). Hecht and Gergle's work suggests that user interests and/or expertise also vary across cultures and languages, as Wikipedians across the globe choose to document knowledge concerning different subjects.

Going beyond *what* is documented, Callahan and Herring (2011) explored cultural differences in *how* knowledge is documented. They constructed a parallel corpus of articles on famous people (Americans and Poles) contributed to the English and Polish Wikipedias. They discovered differences, both along lines of the subject being documented and the language used to do so. They found that American subjects receive more positive coverage as compared to Poles, at both Wikipedias. In addition, their entries often contain information of a personal nature (e.g., their romantic relationships and sexual lifestyle). In terms of writing style, they found that English Wikipedia entries are longer, are written in a more positive tone, and contain more diverse information on the subject as compared to Polish entries.

Callahan and Herring do not interpret these differences as an indication of intentional biases. Rather, they explain that they reflect the economic and political histories of the respective cultures and countries, highlighting that Polish is a small language associated with only one country. Polish Wikipedia is "written by Poles for Polish readers, and they reflect Polish history, values, and concerns" (Callahan and Herring 2011, 1912). We also compare the content of English Wikipedia to that of a small Wikipedia. Like Polish and in contrast to English, Modern Greek is not a global language, being associated only with Greece, Cyprus, and the Greek diaspora. Therefore, we also expect to find that Greek Wikipedia has a local character, and seek to find out if its current events portal emphasizes local values and interests as compared to the portal at the English Wikipedia.

International News Coverage

As mentioned, the observed cultural differences have led some to question whether or not a neutral point of view is possible in a global Wikipedia. Given that the current work focuses on archived news events, we should note that scholars of mass communication have considered the manner in which international events are represented in the media. They have questioned whether or not the news industry presents a balanced picture of the world.

Wu (2000) claims that the media paint a "distorted" picture of the world, since events, people, and places are not represented evenly. Citing Hopkins and Waller-stein (1996), Wu explains that, at the international level, information flows reflect the structure of the global system, where factors including politics, economy, and culture play key roles. In addition, communication infrastructure and resources (e.g., hardware such as satellite facilities, human resources such as international correspondents) likely affect the volume and content of information about any given country in the international news. In his empirical study, Wu found that a country's trade volume and presence of international news agencies were the strongest predictors of the volume of coverage it would receive. Not surprisingly, the United States was the most prevalent country in his data. Given these findings, we expect to observe that even at Greek Wikipedia, news about the United States and other world powers will be prevalent along with news that emphasize local interests and values.

Gatekeeping and News Values

Finally, the concepts of *gatekeeping* and *news values* can help us understand why some events are more likely than others to come to people's attention. As noted by Barzilai-Nahon (2008), the concept of information gatekeeping is used in several fields of study. In the context of communication studies, gatekeeping is seen as a selection process, by which the plethora of available messages gets reduced to a manageable subset, which can reach people during the course of their day (Shoemaker 1991). For instance, journalists and editors make judgments as to which events in the world are important enough to become news. Wikipedians then decide which of these published news events should be recorded in the portal.

When events possess certain "news values" they are more likely to be selected by journalists and editors because they make for an interesting story for audiences (Mc-Quail 2010, 310). Factors such as negativity, drama, and close occurrence to home increase the likelihood that a story will be covered (Galtung and Ruge 1965). However, news values are not universal across cultures (Wilhoit and Weaver 1983). In addition, gatekeepers' judgment of professional news values can be jeopardized when making decisions concerning international stories about one's own country (Nossek 2004). In other words, journalists may be more professional when covering others' news events rather than their own. We might ask what differences there are in terms of news values when we compare the international events logged at the portals. Wiki-pedians may tend to judge news regarding their own country and culture to be more "important" and worthy of recording as compared to news about other countries.

Furthermore, we should also consider how events are represented. *Framing* refers to the manner in which news is contextualized in order to be interpreted by the public (McQuail 2010, 557). Samaras (2005) studied how 9/11 was portrayed in the American versus Greek press. He argues that in the United States, the government's response to 9/11 was typically presented using a "War on Terrorism" frame. To contrast, in the Greek press, a frame emphasizing anti-Americanism was widely used to interpret the aftermath of 9/11. In short, there are significant cultural differences in terms of how international events are represented. Cross-culturally, Wikipedians likely represent events differently, reflected through the choices of articles they cite. We expect that contributors will be likely to choose "their" local news sources in representing current events. By doing so, they frame world events in a manner more relevant to their interests and views as compared to foreign sources.

RESEARCH QUESTIONS

The previous research on cultural differences across Wikipedias, as well as theories surrounding the production of news, suggest that we will observe cultural differences at the current events portals. Therefore, we examine the following research questions:

Q1: What are the salient *news values* observed in the Greek- and English-language current events portals, as evidenced by the news events Wikipedians record?

Q2: How are international news stories *represented*, as evidenced by the choice of citation?

DATA AND METHODS

We study all events recorded by Greek- and English-speaking Wikipedians from 2007 through 2012, a corpus containing over forty-six thousand events. Beginning in 2007, the current events portals at the two communities share a similar structure, with events recorded and displayed in chronological order. Table 3.2 details the volume of events logged. As can be observed, the English portal contains roughly three times as many events as the Greek portal, which is expected given the relative sizes of their user bases. We also observe that in both communities, the number of URLs cited is less than the number of events recorded.

Table 3.2.   Number of Events Recorded, Words Used to Describe Them, and News Sources (URLs) Cited

	English Wikipedia			Greek Wikipedia		
	# Events	# Words	#URLs	# Events	# Words	#URLs
2007	4,184	106,629	4,032	1,681	36,387	1,325
2008	3,207	79,272	2,026	1,668	40,166	1,606
2009	4,447	102,319	4,330	1,864	42,878	1,828
2010	8,551	207,820	8,017	1,817	42,019	1,796
2011	8,314	189,823	7,527	2,555	51,694	2,277
2012	6,284	154,383	5,729	1,681	34,852	1,556
Total	34,987	840,246	31,661	11,266	247,996	10,388

Like Callahan and Herring (2011), we study content differences between two Wikipedias. However, they conducted a manual content analysis, whereas we experiment with statistical techniques that enable us to examine content on a larger scale. Clearly, it would not be feasible to analyze our entire data set using manual methods. Experimentation with statistical techniques will enable us to compare content differences between multiple Wikipedias in future work, as finding methods and tools that do not have inherent English-language biases is a challenge (Krippendorff 2004, 14).

We experiment with a language-independent method, Latent Semantic Analysis (LSA) (Landauer, Foltz, and Laham 1998). LSA derives a set of salient concepts discussed in a body of texts (descriptions of news events, in our case). In particular, it analyzes the co-occurrences of words in order to discover sets of words likely to be related, in the sense that they are used together to describe a concept or theme. The researcher then interprets which concept each set of words represents. As will be demonstrated, LSA is a useful technique for ascertaining which key concepts are discussed in a large body of texts that is too large to code manually.

The analysis will be carried out as follows. In order to address questions related to *news values*, we first compare the distribution of topical labels used at each community (e.g., armed conflicts, politics, sports). These labels are used by Wikipedians (beginning in 2010 and 2011 at the English and Greek communities, respectively) in order to organize events by genre.

Next, we perform LSA on users' textual descriptions of events, exploiting all of our data. We construct a semantic space for each news portal based on the most frequent one thousand words used in event descriptions. Specifically, we count the frequencies of these one thousand words over the recorded news events. This process results in a 34,987 by 1,000 matrix for the English data, and a matrix with dimensions of 11,266 by 1,000 for the Greek data. Each matrix is subjected to a factor analysis, and we retain the factors with eigenvalues greater than one, following the Kaiser criterion (Kaiser 1960). By examining the co-occurrences of words, LSA helps us determine the underlying themes in the news events. We will interpret these themes, guided by the concept of news values as well as the words that are highly correlated to each theme, in order to compare what types of events are important at each community.

Finally, we compare the distribution of information sources that users choose in order to represent events. In particular, we consider the overall diversity of sources used by each community as well as their origin.

ANALYSIS

News Values

To better understand the relationship between the Greek and English Wikipedias, and to shed light on the role of Wikipedias in smaller world languages, we consider the news values that are exhibited in each community. According to Galtung and Ruge (1965, 65), "What we choose to consider an 'event' is culturally determined."

Given that participants are to record *significant, international news events,* an interesting question is whether or not English- and Greek-speaking Wikipedians tend to record different types of events.

Use of Topical Labels

Participants organize events on a given day using topical labels. We can consider the distribution of labels used at each community in order to get an idea as to how often particular genres of news stories are considered important enough to record. From June 2010 to December 2012 at the English Wikipedia, a total of 5,625 topical labels were used. In the Greek community, from January 2011 to December 2012, a total of 1,833 labels were used to categorize news stories. The labels used at the Greek community appear to be close translations of the English labels, with minor differences that did not substantially change their meaning (e.g., "health and medicine" versus "medicine and well-being").

Figure 3.1 shows the distribution of labels at the English and Greek portals. In other words, the figure shows the number of occurrences of a given label, divided by the total number of labels used at the portal. A *z*-test for comparing two population proportions reveals several statistically significant differences (with a *p*-value approaching zero).[9] In the English events, the following labels are used significantly

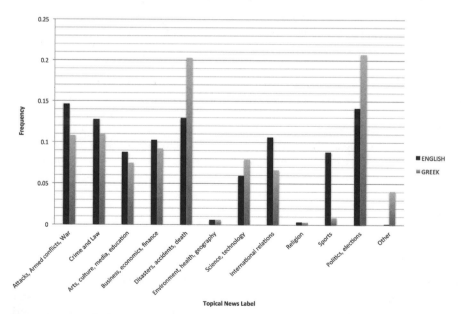

Figure 3.1. Topical news labels.

more often than in the Greek events: *attacks, armed conflicts and war; international relations*; and *sports*. In contrast, Greek Wikipedians use the labels *disasters, accidents, death* and *politics and elections* at greater frequencies.

Latent Semantic Analysis of Event Descriptions

The analysis of labels suggests that there are cultural differences in terms of what genres of news stories are recorded. However, this analysis only considers the labels themselves, not the description of events that participants record or the number of events per category. In addition, the analysis does not make use of all of our data, since labels were not in use before 2010. In order to overcome these limitations and to glean additional insights into each community's news values, we apply LSA to the full set of events recorded.

Tables 3.3 and 3.4 describe the salient dimensions in the texts used to describe events at the English and Greek portals, respectively. As can be seen, LSA uncovered seventeen key themes in the English events, and nineteen in the Greek events. The tables show our interpretation of each factor, the percent of variance in the data accounted for by the given factor, and finally, the set of content words most important to the factor (i.e., with the highest loadings). Words in bold have factor loadings that are greater than 0.5, and words that appear in parentheses have negative loadings (i.e., are negatively correlated to the factor).

In the English data, we observe that the first three factors, as well as the fourteenth factor, concern the Middle East. Taken together, these factors account for almost half of the variance in the data (46.7 percent), indicating that news from the Middle East is a key concern in the English-language community. The Greek-language community also values news about the Middle East, although to a lesser extent. The first four factors here also relate to the Middle East but account for just over 33 percent of the variance in the data.

Another interesting difference is the existence of a theme concerning sports in the English data (the fifth factor, accounting for 6.5 percent of the data's variance), which does not have an equivalent in the Greek data. This confirms the observation from the analysis of topical labels, that English-language Wikipedians more often record news about sports as compared to the Greeks.

As expected, there are differences between the portals with respect to which particular countries are of greatest interest. The United States receives attention from both communities, although more so in the English portal. From the English data, two themes that are clearly related to the United States emerge (F8 and F11). In the Greek data, while we do not observe an equivalent factor, we can see that the United States is an important key word related to several of the underlying themes (e.g., F6, F9, F11). In addition, we observe that news about Greece is key at the Greek community, but not at the English. In particular, in the Greek data, a theme concerning the Greek political and economic crisis is discovered (F13). Finally, we observe that while news related to Russia emerges as a salient factor in both the English and Greek

Table 3.3. Factors Resulting from the Analysis of English Current Events

	Variance	Key words
F1: Middle East	29.8	**Killed, people, nations, Iran, Israel, minister, world, government, capital, president**
F2: Unrest in the Arab world	7.1	**Syria, uprising, league,** capital, former, kingdom, killed, new, Libya, protest
F3: International relations—Libya	6.6	**Libya, protest,** forces, U.S., uprising, war, kingdom, leader, governor, council
F4: Disasters	6.6	**Hurricane, nuclear, earthquake, die, fire, crisis, council, government, state, military**
F5: Sports—football	6.5	**Cup, African,** list, national, football, world, former, republic, police, capital
F6: Elections	5.8	**Election, European, France, governor,** presidential, minister, prime, government, president, party
F7: Russia	4.3	**Georgia, Russia, south,** conflict, hurricane, floods, military, crisis, conflict, northern
F8: United States	4.2	**States, united,** Israel, list forces, kills, hurricane, floods, world, war
F9: Acts of violence, terror	4.0	**Bomb,** general, military, Ireland, U.S., kills, police, state, south, Iraq
F10: Legal matters	3.7	**Over, court,** leader, democratic, European, world, republican, council, union, united
F11: U.S. politics	3.7	**Party,** republican, democratic, hurricane, leader, league, crisis, election, new, national
F12: Violence in Africa	3.6	**Somalia, war,** list, crisis, kills, conflict, republic, united, forces, against
F13: Pakistan	3.6	**Pakistan,** kills, general, state, floods, Russian, prime, court
F14: Iraq	3.2	**Iraq,** war, democratic, Iran, (Ireland), (league), (crisis), (list)
F15: China	2.8	**China, republic,** northern, court, Ireland, council, national
F16: Law enforcement	2.4	**News,** police, world, kingdom, (capital), (presidential), court, uprising
F17: Changes on the international scene	2.1	Against, new, former, (war), union, (kills), cyclone, league

Table 3.4. Factors Resulting from the Analysis of Greek Current Events

	Variance	Key words
F1: Unrest in the Arab world	11.6	**Gaddafi, riots, Libya, government,** protestors, Syria, opposition, countries, civil war
F2: Syrian uprising and resistance	8.4	**People, Syria, win, come from,** (death), (Richter), result, civil war, demonstrations
F3: Iraq	7.1	**Death, conducted,** movie, Iraq, president, United Nations, (wounded), assume, former, (elections)
F4: Middle East violence	6.6	**Israel, Gaza, attack,** result, Russia, life, assume, announce
F5: Politics—elections	6.3	**Elections, parliamentary,** party, United Nations, Afghanistan, (former), parliament, democracy
F6: Russia	5.9	**Georgia, democracy, Russia,** U.S., country, China
F7: Changes on the international scene	5.8	**First, time,** world, Afghanistan, Sudan, Greece, former, parliament, (games)
F8: Disasters	5.5	**Killed, wounded,** people, (United Nations), life, floods, Korea
F9: International relations	5.4	**Country,** U.S., United Nations, (win), (come from), (wounded), death, (life)
F10: Antigovernment demonstrations	5.3	**Demonstrators,** president, announce, countries, Iran, government, Korea, win
F11: Politics abroad	5.0	**President, opposition,** Madagascar, Iran, U.S., government, announce, party, (Greece)
F12: Middle East and Asia	4.3	Korea, Iran, Afghanistan, (Richter), Iraq, (win), (death), (Greece), announce, assume
F13: Greek crisis	4.0	**Crisis, government,** Greece, win, democracy, (death), (people), opposition, party
F14: Elections worldwide	3.7	Elections, prime minister, come from, world, government, parliament, (attack), opposition, (games)
F15: Parliamentary elections	3.6	**Seats** (government), party parliament, win, president, (Nobel), member of parliament
F16: Attacks	3.3	**Attack,** Iraq, (news), (announce), U.S.
F17: Heads of state abroad	3.2	**President,** (opposition), former, government, Nobel, (life), (China), (Greece), U.S.
F18: Africa	2.8	Assume, Madagascar, first, death, Sudan, parliament, world, attack
F19: International	2.5	Life, China, parliament, movie, government, riots, (prime minister), Iran, (death)

data, news related to China, Pakistan, and Iraq is of greater concern to the English-language community.

In summary, our analysis confirms the expectation that there are cross-cultural differences in news values. However, at the same time, we observe that powerful nations (e.g., the United States) and regions of interest to world powers (e.g., China, Russia) are important themes at both communities. Archived current events have passed through two gatekeeping processes—the editorial processes associated with the production of news, and the judgment of Wikipedians creating a collective memory place. In other words, to be recorded in the portal, an event that happens in the world not only needs to make it into the mass media, but also must be valued by Wikipedians at the respective cultural community. In the next section, we will observe further details of the gatekeeping processes at work here, as the analysis of the URLs used by Wikipedians will tell us which sources of news from the mass media they use to document world events.

Representation of Current Events

We now turn to examining the types of URLs that English- and Greek-language Wikipedians use as the most representative sources of recorded events. We ask whether Greek Wikipedia provides local, Greek-language information sources to the community. We begin by considering the domains of the URLs that users cite. We do this because users may not always cite news sources; they may refer to government or educational websites, for instance. Following that, we consider the most-cited news sources in our data.

URLs Cited

We begin by considering the top-level domains of URLs (.com, .gov, .mil, .net, .int, .edu, .org). Three of these are strictly limited to use by entities in the United States (.gov, .mil, and .edu), while the remaining four do not provide definitive information as to the country of origin. Some 55.9 percent of the URLs in the English data set have top-level domains, while in the Greek data the proportion is only 44 percent.

We then consider the URLs that have country codes. We expect to find that Greek Wikipedians will be more likely to cite European sources, and this expectation is confirmed by the findings in table 3.5. As shown, URLs with European country codes are indeed much more frequently cited in the Greek portal as compared to the English-language portal. In addition, if we exclude the United Kingdom, the difference is even more dramatic. Finally, we can consider the use of URLs with the individual country code of Greece (.gr). In the Greek data, 27.7 percent of cited URLs bear this code, as compared to only 0.02 percent of the English URLs. In other words, English-language Wikipedians rarely use Greek sources, even when documenting events that concern Greece (e.g., the ongoing financial crisis).

Table 3.5.   Prevalence of URLs with European Country Codes

	European country codes	*European (excluding .uk)*
English	34%	2.2%
Greek	46%	30%

News Sources Cited

Next, we found the forty most-cited sources within each community. Not surprisingly, as illustrated in figure 3.2, the distribution of news sources cited follows a power law, and this finding holds for both communities. In fact, the most-cited news source in both communities is the British Broadcasting Corporation (BBC), which accounts for 26.8 percent of the citations in the English portal and 12.9 percent of those in the Greek portal. BBC News is the largest broadcast news organization worldwide and is well known for its world news programs.[10] Nonetheless, it is particularly interesting to see that several sources based outside of North America are among the most-cited sources at English Wikipedia.

In the English portal, 2,063 unique sites are cited, as compared to 1,010 at the Greek portal. Nonetheless, it can be said that the Greek portal's citations are more diverse. Here, thirteen news sources account for 50 percent of the URLS cited; at the

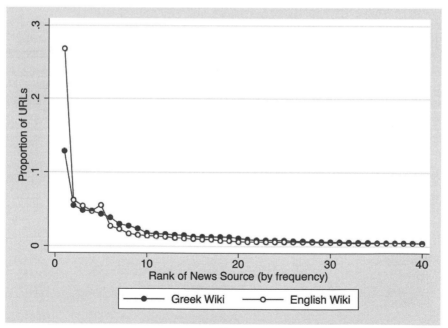

Figure 3.2.   Distribution of sources used follows a power law in both Wikis.

English	Greek
1. BBC	1. BBC
2. Reuters	2. in.gr
3. Al Jazeera	3. Kathimerini
4. Google	4. Reuters
5. CNN	5. Al Jazeera
6. Guardian	6. CNN
7. NYTimes	7. enet.gr
8. ABC Australia	8. e-tipos.com
9. Xinhua	9. Google
10. Washington Post	10. express.gr

Figure 3.3. The ten most-cited sources.

English portal, only six news sources account for half of the URLs used. Figure 3.3 shows the ten most frequently cited sources at each community. As can be seen, the Greek portal features more local sources of news; of the top forty, there are thirteen Greek-language sources.

Finally, table 3.6 breaks down the top forty news sources cited by their respective geographical origins. As can be seen, English Wikipedia features substantially more North American news sources. Likewise, Greek current events are likely to be represented by European sources. Another interesting difference is the English-language community's greater use of Middle Eastern sources. While *Al Jazeera* is among the top forty in both communities, the English-language community also makes frequent use of two Israeli news sources in English (*Jerusalem Post, Haaretz*) as well as the Tehran-based, English-language *Press TV*.

Table 3.6. Top Forty News Sources by Region of Origin

	English		Greek	
	Sources	*% URLs*	*Sources*	*% URLs*
North America	17	0.2264	12	0.1328
Europe	11	0.4167	21	0.4952
Australasia	3	0.0339	4	0.0336
Middle East	4	0.0698	1	0.0434
Asia	4	0.0304	2	0.0182
Africa	1	0.0060	0	0.0000

DISCUSSION

Research on the production of news, as well as on Wikipedia itself, has shown that knowledge about the world is documented and distributed in ways that are not uniform across cultures. We investigated six years of archived current events at the English and Greek Wikipedias. Our findings indicate that there are salient differences, both with respect to the types of news events recorded as well as the information sources selected to represent them. Following Callahan and Herring (2011), we do not attribute the cross-cultural differences to bias or violation of Wikipedia's NPOV. Rather, we view it as natural that Wikipedians' news values are influenced by their dominant culture, and that they want to include events that are "close to home."

Three interesting examples, posted in February 2007, concretely illustrate this point. On February 4, English-language Wikipedians logged the following event: "Greece's conservative government wins a vote of confidence, ending a three-day debate that started with the opposition Socialist Party calling for early elections," citing AP newswire. The equivalent entry at Greek Wikipedia was three sentences long, detailing the number of votes for and against and breaking down the votes cast by political party. In addition to the AP, the Hellenic Broadcasting Corporation (ERT) was cited.

During this month, we also find two examples of "local heroes." Both were indeed international events, but they were not recorded in the English portal. One entry describes a ceremony held at the University of Cairo in honor of two Greek Nobelists, and its news source is *Kathimerini*, a leading Greek newspaper. The second highlights the publication of a scientific study by a team of researchers from the UK and Canada. Of note is that the head of the research team is a Greek (or perhaps Greek Canadian) professor at McGill University, and that the news source cited is Reuters. This event is not recorded in the English portal, despite taking place in North America and appearing in English-language mass media.

As depicted in figure 3.4, we observe that information on world events might take various paths in reaching a given Wikipedia's current events portal, and that there are synergies between Wikipedias. "Our news," depicting happenings in the world that are close to a given community, can end up in "their events"—being recorded in a Wikipedia not particularly close to the event (in terms of geography, culture, or economic and political relations) in a number of ways. For instance, cosmopolitan and/or multilingual individuals might disseminate information to multiple Wikipedias. On the other hand, in the case of a highly unusual news story, it might have made it into the foreign press and could have been noticed and logged by a local Wikipedian. In addition, as noted in the figure, translation tools might also enable users to introduce their news to other Wikipedias, even if they do not speak the language.

Barzilai-Nahon (2008) notes that the concept of *gatekeeping* is understood and applied differently across disciplines. In contrast to gatekeeping as a selection process, some information scientists posit gatekeepers as people who can move between communities and cultures. Such gatekeepers link people with information they

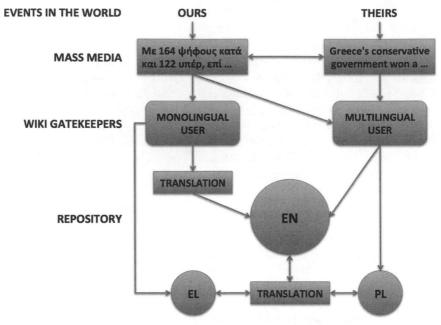

Figure 3.4.   Information flows on current events in global Wikipedia.

would not otherwise encounter (Kurtz 1968). Users who are comfortable navigating multiple cultures and languages, perhaps due to their own backgrounds and/or abilities in exploiting support tools, are likely key in linking a given Wikipedia to information originating from "other" sources.

Role of Smaller Wikipedias

Our findings suggest that the smaller Wikipedias, which place emphasis on local values, have an important role to play. First, their current events portals can bring international news to the local audience, contextualizing it in a way that is meaningful. Events that are close to home are highlighted, and local sources of information are cited. In other words, smaller Wikipedias may function in a similar manner to local news outlets, which help to engage citizens, presenting information in a way that interests them (Moy et al. 2004).

In addition, the current events portal could help reverse the distortion in international news distributed through the mass media. Wu (2000), invoking Marshall McLuhan's concept of the *global village* (McLuhan 1962, 31), calls for "new procedures to improve information flow and international understanding" (Wu 2000,

128). The portals at the smaller Wikipedias can play a role here by providing the global community with local news sources on "their news," which might share more detailed information and/or a different perspective.

Continuing the example above, if an American, noting the brief entry in her native Wikipedia regarding the Greek government's vote of confidence, wanted to learn more about this event, she might learn of Greek sources through the citations at the Greek portal. With the right translation tools, she can access a different point of view on the matter, from a source close to the event. Thus, global Wikipedia enables "niche news" (Hamilton 2004, 192), or a "long tail," a very large inventory of specialized information sources (Anderson 2006, 13). By tapping into resources cross-culturally, users obtain more information on international events of interest, obtaining insiders' advice on which sources to read.

Finally, a global Wikipedia promotes understanding and multiperspectivalism. Many users participate in social technologies with the intent of becoming more cosmopolitan (McEwan and Sobre-Denton 2011). Such users value the opportunity to build social capital across cultures, often developing empathy toward others that transcends their local ties.

CONCLUSION

Our work contributes to a sociotechnical understanding of collaboration in Wikipedia at the macrolevel by examining the similarities and differences in the *content* of the current events portal. We have drawn on literature from information science as well as mass communication in order to propose a view of how smaller and larger Wikipedias interact to comprise a global memory space. Additionally, we have theorized as to why a global Wikipedia matters and the role it might play in reducing distorted views of the world, promoting understanding between cultures. Empirically, we have demonstrated the usefulness of data-driven, language-independent, automated methods for examining content differences between Wikipedias.

In conclusion, the present work demonstrated that the current events portals at smaller and larger Wikipedias both make unique contributions to a global Wikipedia. Encouraging more synergies between Wikipedias would allow for users to zoom in and out, accessing detailed information on events happening around the world as desired. In addition, the presence of smaller Wikipedias helps to maintain balance as far as which international events are remembered and documented over time and how they are represented. Our findings lead us to strongly concur with Callahan and Herring (2011, 1914), who recommend that "Wikipedia content developers should allow linguistic editions to develop organically, rather than seeding them with content from other (especially the English) editions." Rather, we should provide both tools and social incentives to promote cross-cultural synergies between Wikipedias.

66   *Jahna Otterbacher*

NOTES

1. History of Wikipedia, http://en.wikipedia.org/wiki/History_of_Wikipedia.
2. Wikipedia:Multilingual statistics, http://en.wikipedia.org/wiki/Wikipedia:Multi lingual_statistics.
3. Wikipedia:Neutral point of view, http://en.wikipedia.org/wiki/Wikipedia:Neutral_point_of_view.
4. http://en.wikipedia.org.
5. http://el.wikipedia.org.
6. List of Wikipedias, http://meta.wikimedia.org/wiki/List_of_Wikipedias.
7. Editing Portal:Current events/2013 January 28, http://en.wikipedia.org/w/index.php?title=Portal:Current_events/2013_January_28&action=edit&editintro=Portal:Current_events/Edit_instructions.
8. Συζήτηση πύλης:Τρέχοντα γεγονότα, http://el.wikipedia.org/wiki/Συζήτηση_πύλης:Τρέχοντα_γεγονότα.
9. All comparisons of proportions of attributes between the two communities that are reported in the remainder of the paper have been tested using the z-test and are statistically significant differences with a p-value of less than 0.01.
10. BBC News, https://en.wikipedia.org/wiki/BBC_News.

REFERENCES

Anderson, Chris. 2006. *The Long Tail*. New York: Hyperion.
Barzilai-Nahon, Karine. 2008. "Toward a Theory of Network Gatekeeping: A Framework for Exploring Information Control." *Journal of the American Society for Information Science and Technology* 59, no. 9: 1493–1512.
Callahan, Ewa S., and Susan C. Herring. 2011. "Cultural Bias in Wikipedia Content on Famous Persons." *Journal of the American Society for Information Science and Technology* 62, no. 10: 1899–1915.
Ferron, Michela, and Paolo Massa. 2012. "Psychological Processes Underlying Wikipedia Representations of Natural and Manmade Disasters." *Proceedings of WikiSym '12*, Linz, Austria, August 27–29.
Galtung, Johan, and Mari Holmboe Ruge. 1965. "The Structure of Foreign News." *Journal of Peace Research* 2: 64–91.
Halavais, Alexander, and Derek Lackaff. 2008. "An Analysis of Topical Coverage of Wikipedia." *Journal of Computer-Mediated Communication* 13, no. 2: 429–40.
Hamilton, James T. 2004. *All the News That's Fit to Sell: How the Market Transforms Information into News*. Princeton, NJ: Princeton University Press, 2004.
Hara, Noriko, Pnina Shachaf, and Khe Foon Hew. 2010. "Cross Cultural Analysis of the Wikipedia Community." *Journal of the American Society of Information Science and Technology* 61, no. 10: 2097–2108.
Hecht, Brent, and Darren Gergle. 2010. "The Tower of Babel Meets Web 2.0: User-Generated Content and Its Applications in a Multilingual Context." *Proceedings of the Conference on Human Factors in Computer Systems* (CHI). New York: ACM Press.
Hofstede, Geert. 1991. *Cultures and Organizations: Software of the Mind*. London: McGraw-Hill, 1991.

Hopkins, Terence K., and Immanuel Wallerstein. 1996. *The Age of Transition: Trajectory of the World-System, 1945–2025.* Atlantic Highland, NJ: Zed Books.

Jones, Craig O. 2009. "Look it Up in Wikipedia." *Planet Magazine*: 27–31.

Kaiser, Henry F. 1960. "The Application of Electronic Computers to Factor Analysis." *Educational and Psychological Measurement* 20: 141–51.

Kolbitsch, Josef, and Hermann Maurer. 2006. "The Transformation of the Web: How Emerging Communities Shape the Information We Consume." *Journal of Universal Computer Science* 12, no. 2: 187–213.

Krippendorff, Klaus. 2004. *Content Analysis: An Introduction to Its Methodology,* 2nd edition. Thousand Oaks, CA: Sage.

Kurtz, Norman R. 1968. "Gatekeeper: Agents in Acculturation." *Rural Sociology* 33, no. 1: 64–70.

Landauer, Thomas K., Peter W. Foltz, and Darrell Laham. 1998. "An Introduction to Latent Semantic Analysis." *Discourse Process* 25: 259–84.

Leidner, Dorothy E., and Timothy Kayworth. 2006. "A Review of Culture in Information Systems Research: Toward a Theory of Information Technology Culture Conflict." *MIS Quarterly* 30, no. 2: 357–99.

Lih, Andrew. 2004. "Wikipedia as Participatory Journalism: Reliable Sources? Metrics for Evaluating Collaborative Media as a News Resource." *5th International Symposium on On line Journalism*, Austin, Texas.

McEwan, Bree, and Miriam Sobre-Denton. 2011. "Virtual Cosmopolitanism: Constructing Third Cultures and Transmitting Social and Cultural Capital though Social Media." *Journal of International and Intercultural Communication* 4, no. 4: 252–58.

McLuhan, Marshall. 1962. *The Gutenberg Galaxy: The Making of Typographic Man.* Toronto: University of Toronto Press.

McQuail, Denis. 2010. *Mass Communication Theory,* 6th edition. London: Sage.

Moy, Patricia, Michael R. McCluskey, Kelley McCoy, and Margaret A. Spratt. 2004. "Political Correlates of Local News Media Use." *Journal of Communication* 54, no. 3: 532–46.

Nossek, Hillel. 2004. "Our News and Their News: The Role of National Identity in the Coverage of Foreign News." *Journalism* 5, no. 3: 343–68.

Pentzold, Christian. 2009. "Fixing the Floating Gap: The Online Encyclopedia Wikipedia as a Global Memory Place." *Memory Studies* 2, no. 2: 255–72.

Pfeil, Ulrike, Panayiotis Zaphiris, and Chee Siang Ang. 2006. "Cultural Differences in Collaborative Authoring of Wikipedia." *Journal of Computer-Mediated Communication* 12: 88–113.

Samaras, Iathanassios N. 2005. "Représentations du 11-Septembre dans Quatre Journaux Grecs. Une Question de Cadrage." *Questions de Communication* 8: 367–88.

Shoemaker, P. J. 1991. *Gatekeeping.* Newbury Park, CA: Sage.

Wilhoit, G. Cleveland, and David Weaver. 1983. "Foreign News Coverage in Two U.S. Wire Services: An Update." *Journal of Communication* 33, no. 2: 132–48.

Wu, H. Denis. 2000. "Systemic Determinants of International News Coverage: A Comparison of 38 Countries." *Journal of Communication* 50, no. 2: 110–30.

4

Crosslinguistic Neutrality

Wikipedia's Neutral Points of View from a Global Perspective

Ewa Callahan

INTRODUCTION

Neutral point of view (NPOV) is one of the five basic pillars of Wikipedia and one of its core content policies along with verifiability and "no original research." It was first developed for Nupedia by Larry Sanger in 2000 as nonbias policy and was adopted with modifications as Wikipedia policy in 2001. According to this principle, Wikipedia contributors must strive to remain neutral, "representing fairly, proportionately, and as far as possible, without bias, all of the significant views that have been published by reliable sources."[1] This policy relates to both the content as well as the language of the message (what you say and how you say it). Achieving neutrality by avoiding stated opinions and assertions as facts, using nonjudgmental language, and providing relative prominence of opposing views is a responsibility of every contributor. To minimize possible bias, the NPOV policy is explained in details with a number of careful guidelines and tutorials on neutral writing. However, despite all attempts of being simple, straightforward, and in theory, nondebatable, the policy has been heavily discussed in its Talk pages in the English-language Wikipedia. In addition, the number of edits suggests that the concept of neutrality is not self-explanatory. Between February 2002 and November 2011, the policy has been edited 4,500 times by over 1,700 people (Nagar 2012) in the English edition of Wikipedia alone, but the revision process in other linguistic versions is unknown. Currently (July 2013), out of 285 linguistic versions of Wikipedia, at least ninety-two have an article describing Neutral Point of View Policy. Since each of the Wikipedia articles is a living document, actively edited and expanded, several questions arise: Are the documents describing Neutral Point of View Policy similarly among different linguistic versions? How do speakers of languages other than English understand and negotiate the policy? This exploratory chapter will address those questions.

LITERATURE REVIEW

NPOV policy has been the subject of several research studies. One of the most thorough examinations of Wikipedia NPOV policy has been presented by Matei and Dobrescu (2011), who examined how conflict and ambiguity affect the content creation in relation to the NPOV policy. The authors argued that the ambiguity is due to the fact that the rules are open to personal interpretation. In their examination of Talk pages used in the formulation of NPOV, the authors examined how Wikipedia project members are interpreting and negotiating the rules of the policy. The Wikipedia contributors discussed the implementation of the NPOV, considering the fact that NPOV actually encourages not only facts but also opinions. While the establishment of NPOV was designed to provide guidelines and establish clarity, the discussions revealed that different contributors can interpret NPOV policy differently, and that in some cases the discussions actually make the issue more ambiguous. The Talk page contributors outlined possible ways to sidestep the policy by the selective choice of topics of articles or its sections and an uneven support for facts. Some concepts of the policy such as "undue weight"[2] and "prominent adherents"[3] were ambiguous, as the policy is open to interpretation due to lack of clarification of what these terms actually mean. This has resulted in a lengthy debate without specific resolution. However, the authors argue that this ambiguity is the central aspect of Wikipedia, the one that actually makes it work, especially in the areas in which users negotiate NPOV in their own interpretations of the different elements on policy.

Yiftach Nagar (2012), in his research on the collective sense-making process, also examined NPOV edits and Talk pages. Nagar identified several archetypes of questions that people tend to ask about different aspects of the policy to make sense of the way others interpret it. The types of questions include asking for clarification, asking about appropriate behavior (rules), and asking questions as a rhetorical technique before making changes. Differences also have been noted in the answers, varying from offering interpretation, presenting or signaling consensus or disagreement, and explaining to themselves. The exchanges in clarifying the policy not only contribute to sense making but also show commitment to the interpretation of the policy.

The aforementioned publications discuss neutrality of Wikipedia from the perspective of a unified artifact, basing the research on the English-language Wikipedia. Only a handful of social scientists have so far examined the topic of bias and the neutral point of view from a global perspective. Callahan and Herring (2011) examined the neutrality of biographical entries in English- and Polish-language editions of Wikipedia. In their examination of twenty biographical notes, the researchers compared the type of information chosen to describe the life and work of a famous person and language style with consideration on how those choices shape the perception of a person. Their results show substantial differences among the biographies of described subjects, especially in relation to their nationality. Entries of Americans in English-language Wikipedia were very elaborate in comparison with entries for the same people in Polish-language Wikipedia, especially in the area of personal information, family issues, romances, and health. Those entries also had more mentions of controversies as compared with entries in Polish. In contrast, the entries in Polish-language Wikipedia more closely followed the accomplishments of the subject rather than the personal life. Controversial topics are mentioned, but more briefly than in the English-language Wikipedia. One of the interesting characteristics of the Polish-language edition was placing emphasis on the nationality of the subjects, especially Polish nationals, which would confirm the *local heroes* theory (Kolbitsch and Maurer 2006).

In their recent article (2013), Massa and Scrinzi ask if the different linguistic versions of Wikipedia present cultural bias, a phenomenon that can be described as "linguistic point of view." Massa and Scrinzi also call for more detailed (and comparative) analysis of different linguistic versions of Wikipedia to assess the cultural differences between different versions. According to the authors, understanding different linguistic points of view is essential to mutual understanding and harmonious global coexistence.

NEUTRALITY AND BIAS

NPOV has been created to limit possible bias by promoting writing from the neutral perspective. While intentional bias (forcing one's view to gain prominence in the article, despite the presence of alternative views of equal or greater recognition) is more easily noted and discussed, unintentional bias might be created by the fact that people naturally approach issues from their cultural perspective. As Kolbitsch and Maurer (2006) noticed, "Even if an article is written in compliance with the 'neutral point of view' the varying cultural, social, national, and lingual backgrounds can have an enormous influence. Hence, content in Wikipedia can only be as professional and balanced as its authors and their demography are" (196). The issue of cultural perspective has been taken up by a number of researchers (e.g., Kolbitsch and Maurer 2006; Hara, Shachaf, and Hew 2010; Hecht and Gergle 2010; Callahan and Herring 2011). Understanding that culture is an important factor in knowledge building is especially vital when we consider Wikipedia as an entity in the larger sense. While people with a relatively similar cultural background (although it varies depending on how widely the language is spread) edit each of the linguistic versions of Wikipedia, culture can play an even greater role when a topic is presented from two different cultural perspectives.

The Wikipedia community is clearly aware of systemic bias that manifests itself in both the lack of articles on many topics and perspective bias in articles on certain subjects. An article in English Wikipedia titled "Systemic Bias" points out that the bias in the choice of the topics is created due to unequal access to the Internet, English-language ability, availability of sources, and so-called recentism (coverage of most recent events especially in developed English-speaking nations).[4] The

Anglo-American bias of Wikipedia has been identified in its early stages of development, and some scholars such as Reagle (2005) hoped that with the increasing number of international contributors and linguistic versions, criticism that Wikipedia is Anglo-American centric should lessen. While strides have been made to address some of the issues easier to define and regulate such as spellings and place names, the twenty-one types of systemic bias identified in the Wikipedia article "Systemic Bias" will most likely continue, if specific actions are not taken. Attempts to diminish the systemic bias undertaken by WikiProject: Countering Systemic Bias (Livingstone 2010) only cover specific content areas from geographical regions that lack adequate representation in the selection of the articles.

The issues highlighted in the "Systemic Bias" article are certainly valid. However, they are more pronounced if we consider the English-language Wikipedia as a global repository of knowledge. In this case the demography of the editors, their interests, and availability certainly skew the presented view of the world. However, if we consider Wikipedia in a broader sense, as a unit that is composed of different linguistic editions, the coverage bias might be actually smaller, as each of the editions adds the knowledge that might not be available in other language editions. The contributors to the other linguistic editions of Wikipedia are also aware of systemic bias, and at least fifteen linguistic editions have a specific page devoted to this topic.

The bias may also be smaller if we consider it not only from the perspective of the location of the information but also from the access perspective of the user. To any given person the repository of knowledge is limited by physical access to the medium and his or her linguistic ability, so it might not be limited to one version of Wikipedia, making access to information broader, which might limit the bias from the perspective of the reader. Current estimates show that most of the world's population is bilingual/multilingual (Grosjean 2010), and a certain percent can access information in more than one language, even considering that a part of the bilingual/multilingual population speaks languages without written traditions and may not have access to technology. People who can take advantage of multiple linguistic versions of Wikipedia will find a much broader range of information presented from more diverse perspectives. Despite the appearance of a wide overlap of information among the linguistic versions, the intersection in the covered matter is relatively small. According to Hecht and Gergle (2010), who conducted a study on coverage in twenty-five different Wikipedia versions, common encyclopedic knowledge accounts only for one-tenth of 1 percent of content. The small overlap suggests that the coverage bias in Wikipedia in the broadest meaning is actually smaller, as it is viewed just from the English Wikipedia perspective, although more systemic studies on other linguistic versions of Wikipedia are required to confirm or dispute this hypothesis.

NPOV FROM AN INTERNATIONAL PERSPECTIVE

Awareness of the meaning of Neutral Point of View Policy helps eliminate possible bias, but just as with the cultural views of editors that are represented in each article, cultural views may affect understanding of the policy itself. To examine NPOV from an international perspective, one can concentrate on the very text of the NPOV description:

> Achieving what the Wikipedia community understands as neutrality means carefully and critically analyzing a variety of reliable sources and then attempting to convey to the reader the information contained in them fairly, proportionately, and as far as possible without bias. Wikipedia aims to describe disputes, but not engage in them.[5]

The description emphasizes two important points: 1) reliable sources and 2) proportionality. We need to look at both principles from the following perspectives: how they affect English-language Wikipedia, and how they affect Wikipedia as a whole. The NPOV for English Wikipedia states, "Because this is the English Wikipedia, English-language sources are preferred over non-English ones, assuming English sources of equal quality and relevance are available."[6] Although reasonable, this policy misses the opportunity of expanding knowledge by this preference. For many contributors from outside the English-speaking countries, introducing an entry or perspective to English-language Wikipedia presents an opportunity to show it on an international arena. While foreign-language sources are more difficult to access by readers who may not know the language, they might provide important points and present views that otherwise might be missed. We cannot draw a direct comparison between the source that was translated from the original, and, therefore, written from the original cultural perspective, and a source that has been written from the perspective of a foreigner based on his or her own cultural assumptions. The issue is especially complicated if we consider international conflicts or other topics with multiple points of view where sources from all sides would be beneficial to present all or both points of view.

The issue of sources is also applicable to other linguistic versions of Wikipedia. Should we assume that each linguistic version should be based on the sources in its own language? It will most likely not always be the case. For example, the biographics of the Polish-born scientist Maria Curie-Skłodowska, who worked most of her life in France, are based on different sources depending on the language. Out of twenty-eight references in French Wikipedia, eighteen came from French-language sources, seven sources were written in English, one in Italian, one in Polish, and one came from a mixed English/Polish source. Of the seventy-three sources in English-language Wikipedia, sixty-six are in English, six in Polish, and one in French. Eighteen sources in Polish-language Wikipedia are in Polish, although some of them are actually translations of French bibliographies.

The question of the sources also relates to the second principle of NPOV, namely, the proportionality of opinion. According to NPOV policy, the article should include all points of view proportionately. As stated by Jimbo Wales:

- If a viewpoint is in the majority, then it should be easy to substantiate it with reference to commonly accepted reference texts.

- If a viewpoint is held by a significant minority, then it should be easy to name prominent adherents.
- If a viewpoint is held by an extremely small (or vastly limited) minority, it does not belong in Wikipedia regardless of whether it is true or not and regardless of whether you can prove it or not, except perhaps in some ancillary article.[7]

The issue of proper weight should be based on reliable sources, not the opinion of the Wikipedia contributors. This again introduces a potential bias, especially in relation to conflicts. The sources on one side may be different than on the other side, and the majority of one side may be the minority of the other. Additionally, the issue becomes more complicated if we consider the global prominence of languages as introduced by Graddol (1997). Larger languages will have more sources as well as more speakers as a first and second language, making their point of view more prominent, which again introduces potential bias. More sources from the larger languages are also translated into English. The idea of proportional points of view might be, therefore, biased by the popularity of the languages.

These issues raise a number of questions and might be a springboard for future studies. How are majority and minority views understood in a global context? Will those views be negotiated between different linguistic versions of Wikipedia? Or should those views be negotiated in English-language Wikipedia as an international forum? If the points of view are to be presented proportionately, can we accept the fact that the proportions will vary in different linguistic versions? The answer to those questions goes beyond the scope of this chapter, but to highlight the idea of NPOV negotiation on different platforms we can use the example of Nicolaus Copernicus.

The editors of the biographies of Copernicus, the astronomer internationally known for formulating a heliocentric model of the universe, are in constant edit wars over his nationality in Polish and German editions, as both nations tend to claim him as a national hero. The explicit mentioning of nationality has been changed in both versions multiple times, as well as other attributes that would suggest nationality (he was a liege of a Polish king, he signed up to a student organization *Natio Germanorum* at the university in Bologna, his mother came from a German family, most of the printed encyclopedias consider him Polish, etc.). The debates on German Talk pages were so heated that administrators asked contributors to read the archives before raising any more points. Polish Talk pages on this topic are officially closed. The debates contained voices on both sides of the issue and called for the removal of the nationality in his case altogether because agreement could not be reached citing NPOV policy guidelines. Some users opted for different points of view depending on the Wikipedia edition origin: "It is a shame that in Polish Wikipedia it is written that Copernic[us] was German, and here citation, astronomer, it should be Polish and here citation. I am ashamed for a person who wrote that, please someone change that—let Germans write that he was German in the German language Wikipedia" (anonymous, n.d.). While the quote is not in the spirit of NPOV, it raises an important issue of the sources, given written sources for both versions exist depending on the language. It is important to note that the debate over Copernicus and nationality continues on the English-language Wikipedia, which has resulted in a specific (officially disputed) subsection relating to the nationality of Copernicus in his biography. This subsection illustrates once again the arguments for both sides and the failure to resolve the issue.

NPOV POLICIES IN FIFTEEN EDITIONS

Investigation of NPOV policies in various linguistic versions of Wikipedia and associating Talk pages with them can shed some light on the depth in which each linguistic group engages in the policy. To examine the depth of the policy, a sample of the languages was examined comparing the length of the policy and the number of distinct sections. The same counts were conducted on Talk pages to estimate the engagement of the particular community in policy development. Since languages use different writing systems, the pages have been translated into English, using Google translation service, and the counts were conducted on the translated pages. The table below presents data for each policy for fifteen different languages, divided into three groups following Graddol's (1997) linguistic typology (regional languages of major trade blocs—Arabic, Chinese, English, French, German, Russian, Spanish; national languages; and local languages with varying degrees of official recognition). The languages in the first category follow the languages identified by Graddol as regional, except for English. The second category consists of national languages from the first twelve linguistic editions of Wikipedia in the number of articles.[8] The list has been additionally supplemented for comparison by two local languages that are represented in Google Translator. The data were collected in June and July 2013.

As we can see when examining the data, the depth of engagement in the policy itself varies significantly among the languages (see table 4.1). The size of the language does not necessarily directly correspond with the broader explanation of the policy, either. Among the different linguistic groups, it is the national language group that tends to have the most detailed pages presenting the policy; however, it is a tendency rather than a unified trend. The debates on the Talk pages show a different pattern with the languages representing various languages from the global group (Russian, French, and Spanish), although even here Dutch Talk pages contained the most discussions. Talk pages for NPOV in Russian-language Wikipedia have the largest number of threads in spite of the fact that the NPOV policy page is quite short. It contains an explanation of the original description of the policy by Jimbo Wales, followed by five specific examples presenting statements that do not follow the policy and the ways to correct them. The major areas described by the article are scientific style of reporting, credibility, links, and incompleteness. The languages also vary in the way they incorporate the translation from the original article from English Wikipedia, adjusting it to the cultural realm. For example, the Chinese Wikipedia

Table 4.1. Word Count and Section Count for NPOV and Associated Talk Pages

Type	Language	Wikipedia No.	Estimated number of speakers*	NPOV # of words	NPOV # of sections (with subsections)	Talk Pages # of words	Talk Pages # of sections (with subsections)
Regional	Chinese	13	1,197,392,400	6,106	9 (26)	4,309	13 (13)
	Spanish	7	405,638,110	1,741	4 (6)	10,417	13 (13)
	English	1	334,800,758	5,055	9 (30)	108,5972 (in 45 archives)	varies by archive
	Arabic	24	223,010,130	1,037	4 (7)	102	1 (1)
	Russian	8	161,727,650	1,491	7 (12)	16,300	36 (36)
	German	3	83,812,810	2,347	4 (12)	1,827	5 (5)
	French	4	68,458,600	2,246	6 (13)	15,452	8 (8)
National	Portuguese	5	202,468,100	1,857	5 (8)	10,226	18 (18)
	Japanese	10	122,072,000	6,545	14 (19)	6,388	10 (10)
	Vietnamese	11	67,762,060	4,809	6 (21)	1,139	4 (4)
	Italian	6	61,068,677	814	3 (4)	14,734	24 (34)
	Polish**	9	39,042,570	1,390 + 6,445	5 + 9 (21)	5,691 + 4,919	12 (16) + 4 (5)
	Dutch	2	22,984,690	2,278	7 (9)	32,322	19 (33)
	Swedish	12	8,381,829	2,294	5 (17)	516	6 (6)
Local	Catalan	17	7,220,420	1,236	5 (6)	190	1 (1)
	Welsh	64	536,890	1,071	1 (4)	0	0

* Language numbers estimates according to M. Paul Lewis, Gary F. Simons, and Charles D. Fennig, eds., *Ethnologue: Languages of the World*, 17th edition (Dallas, TX: SIL International, 2013). Online version: http://www.ethnologue.com.

** Polish-language Wikipedia, as explained later in the chapter, has two pages outlining the policy, and numbers for both are included in the table.

page still includes passages about Anglo-American bias avoidance while in the Polish version those passages have been substituted with a section on Polonocentrism (Callahan and Herring 2011). Additionally, examples relating to U.S. pop culture were substituted/supplemented with examples from Polish culture (*Mickiewicz was a great poet, Wałęsa was a lame president*) throughout the text.

The discrepancy among the numbers for different linguistic groups may be explained by several factors. The length of the policy may vary depending on what the article editors considered as essential to present to their respective communities, but they also may depend on the cultural preferences in information organization. Some cultures may have tendencies to prefer shallow hierarchies of information, presenting as much as possible on the first page, while others may prefer deep hierarchies when more information follows on the subsequent pages. For example, Sweden's policy is short; however, each section directs the reader to a more detailed page on a specific aspect. The different preferences are also visible in the structure of the pages themselves, with some languages discussing issues in multiple subsections and others discussing a smaller number of issues in more depth. The numbers relating to the NPOV Talk pages also present interesting observations for debate. In the case of regional languages, where the cultural differences are more pronounced despite the common language, the negotiations among the different cultural groups may add to the debate. In the case of the national languages, where the culture is more homogeneous, the debates may ensure that the needs of the particular group are met and the differences relating to particular national/cultural identity are incorporated in the policy.

The raw numbers presented in the table might provide a better understanding of the scope of the issue, but more content-related studies by native speakers are needed to understand the particular areas of importance and conflict in each of the languages. A metastudy in this regard would be beneficial.

NPOV IN POLISH WIKIPEDIA

The question of how the different linguistic communities structure and interpret the NPOV is crucial to understanding Wikipedia in the broad sense as a collection of multiple editions and as a repository of global human knowledge. The depth of the articles outlining the NPOV policy in linguistic editions vary by the length and the level of details and by how much of the article is a translation from the English version and how much of the content is produced by the language community. Using the methodology of Matei and Dobrescu (2011), we can examine the Talk pages to see how different communities adopt the policy and which aspects of the policy they find difficult to interpret.

To illustrate the differences in the interpretation, let's take a look at Polish-language Wikipedia and the Talk pages for the policy formulation. The Polish-language Wikipedia is an interesting example of a community that took over the development of

NPOV from the cultural perspective. As of July 2013, Polish-language Wikipedia is in ninth place in the number of articles among the linguistic versions of Wikipedia, and it is the largest for a language that is official in one country only. It has been consistently in the top ten editions of Wikipedia. For several years, it held fourth place in terms of the number of articles. Started in September 2001 as an independent project, Polish-language Wikipedia was incorporated into Wikipedia in January 2002.[9] Work on NPOV started in December 2002, first as a translation from the English version and then modified by Polish editors. Interestingly, Polish-language Wikipedia has two pages for NPOV: one shorter page describing what the early contributors considered the essence of NPOV,[10] and another, more detailed page (described as a *full version*) that presents all major aspects of the policy.[11] The official NPOV page contains only four short sections: *Explanation of Neutral Point of View, Description of Cultural Artifacts, Two Approaches to Neutrality*, and *Issues of Rule Violations*, which could suggest that those four aspects of the policy were chosen as crucial to understanding the policy. The page informs the reader about the existence of the full version, yet it is the short version that is connected to its English counterpart.

The Talk pages for both versions provide some history about the page creation in 2002. The original text of the neutral point of view was translated from the English version by two contributors: Polimerek and Youandme. The NPOV Talk pages document and inform the reader about the decision to create two different pages. According to the editors, the English-language description of the policy is unnecessarily long. Polimerek writes: "Some parts are excessively verbose IMHO (in particular in response to the allegations). For example, the part about the difference between opinion and fact is also overly developed, while at the same time does not explain what is the actual difference between them (the fact is an objective finding of a state of affairs, and the opinion is a value judgment), although I translated it quite literally, by adding only the sentence distinction."[12] Youandme is in full agreement with the existence of two versions: "This was my plan: to translate everything as faithfully as possible with regard to Polish cultural reality, then publish it, and then work on a shortened version. Short version would be the basic version, so as not to scare newbies with the volume of text."[13]

While the presence of two versions of NPOV seems to have worked at the beginning, in recent years contributors again addressed this topic, suggesting new names for the pages to outline their content (*full version, abridged version*, or even jokingly *version for lazy readers*). The debate continued as the contributors wanted to avoid the situation that other pages of Wikipedia content also have abridged versions. Despite the critical opinions, both versions still exist as of July 2013.

The preference for a shorter version may find explanation in Polish cultural attitudes. In Polish culture overexplanation may be considered patronizing. The succinctness of definitions in Polish encyclopedias dates to the anecdotal entry in the first Polish encyclopedia, where the definition of the horse was simply explained: *How does a horse look like everybody can see* (Chmielowski 1745). This sentence, applied to Polish popular culture, is used to describe concepts that do not require definition or explanation. The preferences for the short and concise articles may also be explained using Edward Hall's (Hall and Hall 1990) concepts of high- and low-context cultures. The Polish language is considered high context (Zięba 2008), meaning that a lot of communication is not verbal, especially in a context in which all speakers share the same background. With regard to rules, Polish culture is particularistic rather than universalistic (Trompenaars and Hampden-Turner 1998; Nawojczyk 2006). Because of lack of independence during the time of partitions in the nineteenth century and a communist rule in the twentieth century, formal rules are often perceived as elements of control and limitation rather than as an instrument established to serve a common good (Nawojczyk 2006).

While this debate over the existence of two versions of the NPOV page was one of the most prominent on the Talk pages, other issues related to the clarification in understanding of the policy. Questions and understanding of neutrality were raised by several contributors, addressing both systemic and proportional bias and even criticizing the Wikipedia administrators for promoting less valuable entries as well as accusing them of censorship.

The neutrality and unemotional reporting is also questioned in cases of criminals. Another contributor, Aung, writes, "There is series of texts about criminals—it is written this way, like the author does not know that it is important to judge a guy who walked in to the class and killed a dozen kids. For a wise person it is enough, but what if an idiot reads that article and thinks, this killed 12 people and it is a subject of encyclopedia article, I will kill 20 and also will be famous. Is this kind of neutrality wise?"[14]

One of the longer debates related to the word *znany*, which can be translated as "famous, well known" and as "known," and the conjunction word *aż*, with many meanings (until, till, before, even, so that). The discussion seemed to be generated by the fact that those words were sometimes automatically removed, without regard for the context of the word. The discussion attracted both opponents and proponents of the word *famous* and was connected to one of the four topics covered in the short version *Description of Cultural Artifacts*. While a number of the discussion participants suggested that the word should be used only when absolutely necessary, there were also several voices in defense of the word *famous*. One of the arguments related to the nature of Wikipedia and the fact that biographies include both really famous people as well as people of regional/low fame; thus, the word *famous* could help people see the differences. One of the contributors (Piotr967) pointed out that while fame might be judged on the basis of accomplishments, people may have difficulties actually judging the prestige of the awards: "Aside from Nobel prize there are many other awards, for example in the field of literature. Some are prestigious; others are awards for the playground friends. It is difficult to differentiate for a layman. Therefore the word famous is needed."[15]

Similarly to the English-language Wikipedia, the Talk pages have a debate about "due and undue weight." However, the discussion here is much shorter. The translator named Bulwersator posts here the whole translated version of the page, asking for approval before moving it to the actual page. While this does not provide the discussion, it sheds light on the process of negotiating the policy. Even though the policy on the main page can be changed, updated, or corrected by other contributors, placing it in the Talk page asking for agreement on translation shows the sensitivity to other major contributors to avoid edit wars later.

Polonocentrism was also a topic of discussion, mostly in the area of clarity of the article and to gain a better understanding of NPOV in the case of the lists that present specific achievements (for example, in sports) by country, where the standing of Polish participants is highlighted. This is especially important because Polish Wikipedia entries are, according to Callahan and Herring (2011), characterized by the more frequent presence of lists than the English-language edition.

In addition to the debates concerning the NPOV policy, the Talk pages have been used to debate the POV of other articles. The longest discussion was related to a topic of natural family planning, which in a country that is predominantly Catholic is a controversial issue and was already heavily discussed in the Talk pages for that topic. Other off-topic points related to articles that discussed historic and ethnic topics (Upper Silesia plebiscite, slang expression for people of different groups that are not neutral by nature, denominations, the Katyń Massacre). Most of the points were raised by Aung, who also made an important point on geographical locations, noting that descriptions of a number of Polish cities, towns, and objects also have German names included, which considering the history of conflicts between both countries may not be desirable.

To gain an even better understanding of the importance of specific aspects of NPOV, it would be beneficial to look at the Polish Neutral Point of View Policy pages from the perspective of specific changes. Since 2002, the NPOV page in English and Polish versions have undergone a number of changes, so it is difficult to differentiate without extensive analysis what is the result of translations and what is the result of the addition/omission on the part of Polish-language contributors. However, the choices that have been implemented in both texts could give a glimpse of how the policy is understood and what aspects are taken with most criticism.

CONCLUSION

When we look at Wikipedia from the perspective of a compilation of linguistic editions and all the world's knowledge it encapsulates, we ought to see it as a whole that is more than just the sum of its parts. It is constructed based on collective knowledge and on the cultural richness of the world, a fact that has been noted by researchers and Wikipedia contributors alike. The issues of systemic and perspective bias observed in the English-language Wikipedia are also present in other editions and contributions, although the types of bias vary depending on the type of linguistic group, with national groups exhibiting stronger tendencies toward cultural self-promotion. As is the case of English Wikipedia, neutral point of view is a concept that is ambiguous and defined somewhat differently in the linguistic contexts, as each language presents a specific challenge of reporting, depending on nuances that may not be easily translatable. The nuances in cultural understanding of bias and neutrality are important, not only in the perception of cultural differences but also in cultural overlap.

This chapter introduced the idea of cultural difference in understanding with consideration to NPOV. The analysis tentatively suggests that there are differences in how different linguistic communities presented and debated the NPOV, although the issue certainly requires more content-related studies with a larger sample of languages. Those studies can also provide answers to a larger array of questions about bias and neutrality from a cultural perspective. Is bias different in various linguistic editions? Is neutrality understood equally in all cultures and defined equally in all linguistic versions of Wikipedia? If differences in the understanding of the definitions are present, do they contribute to or alleviate cultural bias?

Based on the example of Polish Wikipedia, we may suspect that other linguistic editions also prioritize the issues and concepts relative to their culture and understanding of the world. Wikipedia editors are aware of this pattern, although only a handful of Wikipedia editions seem to have a "Systemic Bias" page based on the one in English-language Wikipedia, possibly because the English-language page is not easily culturally translatable. The issue is often discussed in the context of NPOV and bias avoidance rather than the direct projects to offset the systemic bias. Similar to bias, neutrality might also be understood differently among cultures. Based on evaluating NPOV policies, there appear to be large discrepancies in the policy coverage. This does not necessarily mean that some cultures treat neutrality as less important, but rather see the concept less or more ambiguous, as it can be seen from the examples of the Talk pages.

The question—If the difference in the understanding of the definitions are present, do they contribute to or alleviate cultural bias?—is more complex to understand, since we would have to consider the cultural, linguistic, and historical background of Wikipedia contributors, as well as where they choose to negotiate their points of view: the Wikipedia of their native language, another linguistic version of Wikipedia that presents the point of view contrary to their beliefs, or English-language Wikipedia as an international forum. However, with our current state of knowledge, the answer to this question and a deeper understanding of the issues highlighted in this article are not fully possible, suggesting the need for more comprehensive, multischolar studies.

NOTES

1. Wikipedia:Neutral point of view, http://en.wikipedia.org/wiki/Wikipedia:Neutral_point_of_view.

2. In Wikipedia the concept of *undue weight* refers to a situation in which the minority view is described in the same level of details as a majority view, therefore suggesting that both views are equal.

3. In NPOV, identification of *prominent adherents* is needed to present a significant minority view in order for the view to be included in the article.

4. Wikipedia:Systemic Bias, https://en.wikipedia.org/wiki/Wikipedia:Systemic_bias.

5. Wikipedia:Neutral point of view.

6. Wikipedia:Verifiability, https://en.wikipedia.org/wiki/Wikipedia:Verifiability.

7. Wikipedia:Neutral point of view.

8. List of Wikipedias, http://en.wikipedia.org/wiki/List_of_Wikipedias.

9. Polish Wikipedia, http://en.wikipedia.org/wiki/Polish_Wikipedia.

10. Dyskusja Wikipedii:Neutralny punkt widzenia, http://pl.wikipedia.org/wiki/Dyskusja_Wikipedii:Neutralny_punkt_widzenia.

11. Dyskusja Wikipedii:Neutralny punkt widzenia (pełna wersja), http://pl.wikipedia.org/wiki/Dyskusja_Wikipedii:Neutralny_punkt_widzenia_(pełna_wersja).

12. Dyskusja Wikipedii:Neutralny punkt widzenia.

13. Dyskusja Wikipedii:Neutralny punkt widzenia.

14. Dyskusja Wikipedii:Neutralny punkt widzenia (pełna wersja).

15. Dyskusja Wikipedii:Neutralny punkt widzenia (pełna wersja).

REFERENCES

Callahan, Ewa, and Susan C. Herring. 2011. "Cultural Bias in Wikipedia Articles about Famous Persons." *Journal of the American Society for Information Science and Technology* 62, no. 10: 1899–1915.

Chmielowski, Benedykt. 1745. *Nowe Ateny*.

Graddol, David. 1997. *The Future of English?* The British Council.

Grosjean, Francois. 2010. *Bilingual Life and Reality*. Cambridge, MA: Harvard University Press.

Hall, Edward T., and Mildred R. Hall. 1990. *Understanding Cultural Differences*. Yarmouth, ME: Intercultural Press.

Hara, Noriko, Pnina Shachaf, and Khe Foon Hew. 2010. "Cross-Cultural Analysis of the Wikipedia Community." *Journal of the American Society for Information Science and Technology* 61, no. 10: 2097–2108.

Hecht, Brent, and Darren Gergle. 2010. "The Tower of Babel Meets Web 2.0." In *Proceedings of the SIGCHI Conference on Human Factors in Computing Systems*. Atlanta, GA: ACM Press, 291–300. doi:10.1145/1753326.1753370.

Kolbitsch, J., and H. Maurer. 2006. "The Transformation of the Web: How Emerging Communities Shape the Information We Consume." *Journal of Universal Computer Science* 12, no. 2: 187–213.

Livingstone, Randall M. 2010. "Let's Leave the Bias to the Mainstream Media: A Wikipedia Community Fighting for Information Neutrality." *M/C Journal* 13, no. 6.

Massa, Paolo, and Federico Scrinzi. 2013. "Manypedia: Comparing Language Points of View of Wikipedia Communities." *First Monday* 18, no. 1. doi:10.5210/fm.v18i1.3939. http://www.uic.edu/htbin/cgiwrap/bin/ojs/index.php/fm/article/view/3939.

Matei, Sorin Adam, and Caius Dobrescu. 2011. "Wikipedia's 'Neutral Point of View': Settling Conflict through Ambiguity." *The Information Society* 27, no. 1: 40–51. doi:10.1080/019 72243.2011.534368.

Nagar, Yiftach. 2012. "What Do You Think?" In *Proceedings of the ACM 2012 Conference on Computer Supported Cooperative Work* (CSCW '12). New York: ACM, 393–402. doi:10.1145/2145204.2145266.

Nawojczyk, Maria. 2006. "Universalism Versus Particularism through the European Social Survey Lenses." *Acta Physica Polonica B* 37, no. 11: 3059–69.

Reagle, Joseph. 2005. "Is the Wikipedia Neutral?" http://reagle.org/joseph/2005/06/neutrality .html.

Trompenaars, Fons, and Charles Hampden-Turner. 1998. *Riding the Waves of Culture: Understanding Cultural Diversity in Global Business*, 2nd edition. New York: McGraw-Hill.

Zięba, Anna. 2008. "Language and Culture. Verbal Communication in Selected Polish, British and American TV Programmes." *Investigationes Linguisticae* 16.

5

Gender Gap in Wikipedia Editing

A Cross Language Comparison

Paolo Massa and Asta Zelenkauskaite

INTRODUCTION

According to various surveys, the percentage of women editing Wikipedia barely reaches 10 percent.[1,2] The issue of gender distribution on Wikipedia was first brought to public attention by an article in the *New York Times* on January 2011. The article, titled "Define Gender Gap? Look Up Wikipedia's Contributor List,"[3] started by highlighting how, in just ten years, the Wikipedia community accomplished some remarkable goals, such as reaching more than 3.5 million articles in English and starting an online encyclopedia in more than 250 languages. Yet Wikipedia failed to reach at least a minimal gender balance: according to the United Nations and Maastricht University 2010 reported survey, less than 13 percent of contributors were female. A more recent survey carried out in 2011 by the Wikimedia Foundation, the nonprofit organization that coordinates the various Wikipedia projects,[4] reported even a steeper gender gap: women account for just 9 percent of editors.

The importance of Wikipedia editors' diversity is relevant since Wikipedia is increasingly becoming one of the most accessed Web sources for information needs. Some 53 percent of American Internet users searched for information on Wikipedia as of May 2010; 88 percent of 2,318 university students used Wikipedia during a course-related research process, and finally, Wikipedia is the sixth most visited site on the entire Web.[5] Thus, because so many people read the content of Wikipedia pages, it is important to become aware that these pages reflect the point of view of a predominantly male population. This issue has also been addressed by the Wikimedia Foundation, and in fact they have devoted attention to gender balance on Wikipedia as one of the key points of their five-year strategic plan of 2010: "Doubling the percentage of female editors to 25 percent by 2015."[6]

In light of this pronounced gender gap, since 2011 a number of studies have tried to understand the reasons and the extent of this phenomenon in Wikipedia.[7, 8, 9, 10] Yet the challenge of comprehending and improving the situation is still lingering and unsolved.

This study focuses on the extent of the gender gap across various language editions of Wikipedia. Unlike the majority of studies on Wikipedia that predominantly focused on the English Wikipedia, this study uses a cross-cultural and crosslinguistic approach to investigate a mosaic of Wikipedias and sociolinguistic cultural practices that developed over the years, given that as of 2013 there are more than 280 Wikipedia language editions. Yet in this study we consider the English Wikipedia as a reference point, given that it is the oldest, the largest, and the most researched one.

The motivating questions are hence: Is the gender gap in other language editions of Wikipedia as pronounced as it is in the English one? Are there Wikipedia language editions with a narrower or wider gender gap?

The goal of this study is to make a contribution to a better understanding of cross-cultural and crosslinguistic varieties of Wikipedia as continuing the seminal research in this area.[11, 12] Wikipedia provides us a unique context to study the sociocultural differences across language editions, given that they all share a constant element—the MediaWiki open source platform, which serves as a sort of controlled variable. Therefore, the differences found among the different editions of Wikipedia should be due to the different communities of practice inhabiting them and their cultural and historical differences. From this perspective, Wikipedia exhibits advantages to analyze differences among communities. Compared to an analysis of user behaviors across different platforms such as Facebook and Twitter, it keeps the platform as a constant variable.

This study is guided by two research questions:

RQ1: What is the percentage of users who set their gender in different language editions of Wikipedia?

RQ2: Among those who express gender, what percentages comprise female and male contributors?

Our analytic approach is based on data about gender explicitly entered by registered users of Wikipedia. In fact, in the MediaWiki software since 2010 it is possible to express gender in the preferences panel. Yet gender in English Wikipedia is referred to as an optional field, and the template notifies that it is "used for gender-corrected addressing by the software. This information will be public."

METHOD

Wikipedia, as a sociotechnical system,[13] is based on a unified technological platform—MediaWiki—that serves as a basis for all languages editions. Moreover, all

Wikipedias share the same set of established rules and core policies such as the neutral point of view.[14] However, each platform in its language represents a singular, independent case, characterized by specific sociotechnical variables: cultural settings, year of creation, number of registered and active users, and customization of the settings of the platform.

To answer the research questions of this study, we created an automated script querying the replicated databases of Wikipedia that are made available on Toolserver (http://www.toolserver.org) and released it as open source.[15] For every Wikipedia language edition, the script computes the number of registered users, the number of users who expressed their gender, and the number of users who indicated male or female. The percentage of users expressing their gender and the percentage of males and females over those who expressed their gender are computed as well.

We considered only users who registered after January 1, 2010, by setting a parameter of the script. The reason behind this choice is that the gender-setting functionality—the core phenomenon that we are addressing—had been introduced in most Wikipedias in early 2010.

The results refer to the situation as of March 16, 2013. The script produced a list of 289 language editions of Wikipedia. However, many of them had very few users, and in order to conduct reasonable quantitative investigations based on the number of users who expressed their gender, we arbitrarily decided to consider only editions with at least twenty thousand registered users, and this filtering step reduced our sample to seventy-six Wikipedias.

In this contribution we consider the English Wikipedia as a baseline because it was the first to start, and it has the largest number of users, pages, and edits.[16] Moreover, according to the editor survey carried out by the Wikimedia Foundation in 2011,[17]

> An overwhelming majority of Wikipedia editors read and edit English Wikipedia—which also has the largest and most diverse pool of editors, as editors from other projects contribute regularly. In total, 76% of Wikipedia editors contribute to English Wikipedia, although only 40% primarily contribute to English Wikipedia. In other words, in addition to the 40% of editors who primarily edit English Wikipedia, 36% of editors from other language projects contribute to English Wikipedia. An impressive 93% of Wikipedia editors read English Wikipedia, and about half of them (49%) primarily read English Wikipedia. We can clearly see that editors who work mainly in other language projects help English Wikipedia grow.

USERS SPECIFYING THEIR GENDER IN DIFFERENT LANGUAGE EDITIONS OF WIKIPEDIA

The first research question refers to the percentage of users who set their gender in different language editions of Wikipedia. Table 5.1 shows the language editions that have a larger percentage of users expressing their gender.

Table 5.1. Wikipedias with the Largest Percentages of Users Setting Their Gender

Language (Wikipedia web address)	Percentage of users setting their gender	Number of users who set their gender	Number of users
Russian (ru.wikipedia.org)	22.58%	139,038	615,690
Vietnamese (vi.wikipedia.org)	10.54%	18,090	171,568
Ukrainian (uk.wikipedia.org)	9.43%	10,969	116,378
Thai (th.wikipedia.org)	9.12%	7,869	86,321
Portuguese (pt.wikipedia.org)	8.72%	39,499	453,229
Turkish (tr.wikipedia.org)	8.40%	17,370	206,750
Arabic (ar.wikipedia.org)	8.16%	29,143	357,296
Marathi (mr.wikipedia.org)	7.53%	1,820	24,163
Japanese (ja.wikipedia.org)	7.49%	25,428	339,637
Chinese (zh.wikipedia.org)	7.14%	44,796	627,058
Farsi (fa.wikipedia.org)	6.59%	11,917	180,908
Tamil (ta.wikipedia.org)	6.43%	2,258	35,105
Indonesian (id.wikipedia.org)	6.43%	19,319	300,673
....			
English (en.wikipedia.org)	4.85%	353,056	7,283,226

At first glance, the overall small percentage in relation to gender specification stands out. Russian Wikipedia (22.58 percent) in table 5.1 is an outlier, compared to the rest of the language editions. The second in the ranking in table 5.1, the Vietnamese Wikipedia, drops the rate of gender identification to 10.54 percent, maintaining the decreasing pattern in gender self-identification throughout the rest of table 5.1. These results are contrastive, compared to social networking sites such as Facebook on which almost everybody (93.8 percent according to Lampe, Ellison, and Steinfeld[18] and 97 percent according to Stecher and Counts[19]) set the gender. On the other hand, in Wikipedia this practice is less common. On the English Wikipedia, just 4.85 percent of users who registered since 2010 expressed their gender, precisely 353,056 out of 7,283,226.

One possible reason behind a small percentage of users expressing their gender when compared to, for example, Facebook is that the link to the page for changing the gender is not very visible in the interface. The user should first click on "Preferences" and then set their gender on this page.

More importantly there are no clear and visible effects or benefits of setting your gender on Wikipedia. In the interface, it is written that the gender information is optional, and it is "used for gender-correct addressing by the software." Note also the additional text, "this information will be public," has been present since 2010 in the interface (at least in the English Wikipedia). It is not precise since it is unclear when this information will become public, and it is actually incorrect since there are, and have been, different ways to obtain gender-setting information; for example, using the official Wikipedia API, as the WikiTrip web tool does.[20] Thus, there are no clear benefits of setting your gender on Wikipedia, and, contrary to social networking sites such as Facebook, the social aspect of Wikipedia Is Not predominant at all. For example, the policy page "What Wikipedia Is Not" clearly states: "Wikipedia is not a social networking service like Facebook or Twitter. . . . Wikipedians have their own user pages, but they should be used primarily to present information relevant to working on the encyclopedia. Limited biographical information is allowed, but user pages should not function as personal webpages."[21]

The question that remains unanswered is why on some Wikipedias there are larger percentages of users expressing their gender. The reasons are many, but the main ones have to do with the interface. Some languages (due to grammatical rules) highlight gender, referring to users as "she-user" or "he-user." This is, for example, the case in the Russian Wikipedia, which also happens to be the first in table 5.1 with 22.58 percent of users expressing their gender. Moreover, in some of the Wikipedias in table 5.1, the user page has different addresses based on the self-declared gender; for example, in the Portuguese Wikipedia (fifth in table 5.1), male users have their page prefixed by *Usuário* while female users by *Usuária*. In this way, it is possible to hypothesize that users who see these differences become aware of this option and have more incentives in setting their gender.

Interestingly enough, the blog post "Nine Reasons Women Don't Edit Wikipedia (in Their Own Words)" by Wikimedia director Sue Gardner reports that "some women whose primary language has grammatical gender find being addressed by Wikipedia as male off-putting." From a female Portuguese Wikipedian: "I have no problem with the male 'Usuário' (in portuguese). And sincerely, I don't think the fact of see a male word will push me out Wikippedia. We are quite used to use a male word in portuguese when we don't know the gender of someone, but yes, would be nice to see a 'Usuária' in my page :D."[22]

On the other hand, in English there isn't a male and female version of the term *User*, adjectives referred to the active user do not differ based on gender, and "there's only one message in English which is gender-customized."[23]

From the interface point of view, the platform is customizable by authorized users, specifically administrators of a given Wikipedia language edition. For most of the Wikipedias in table 5.1, for which a larger portion of registered users expressed their gender, we note that the "welcome message" interface page they receive after they register is very simple (see figure 5.2). It merely contains an invitation and a link to change their preferences and leads to the preference page in which they can also set their gender. On the other hand, the welcome page on the English Wikipedia (figure 5.1) does not present a link to the preferences page but is mainly focused on suggesting content pages to the user that he or she can start contributing to.

Therefore, based on differences that are exposed in figure 5.1 and figure 5.2, we argue, it would be possible to predict that configuration choices made by individual Wikipedias having an impact on the interface might influence the ways in which users perceive the importance of the gender setting. It is during the new user registration process that it is most likely for users to access this setting, if it is clearly visible.

Welcome to Wikipedia, Useryser!
Looking for an easy way to get started? Just choose a page from one of the three lists below.
Fix grammar & spelling
Khánh Thy
Count of Boulogne
Improve clarity
Windows Internet Name Serv...
Television timeout
Collaborative process autom...
Link pages together
Telman Aliyev
Agricultural protection zoning
Evangel Christian School (Al...
← No thanks, go back to where I was

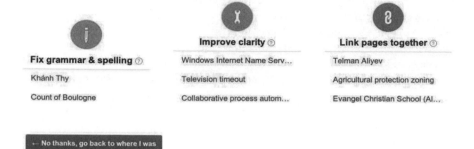

Figure 5.1. Screenshot of the page after creating a new user on English Wikipedia.

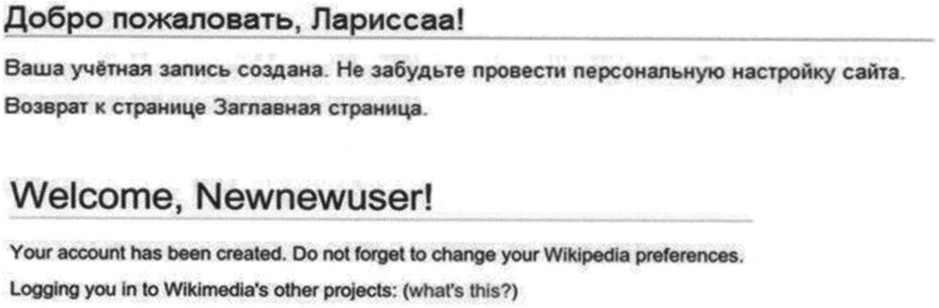

Добро пожаловать, Лариссаа!
Ваша учётная запись создана. Не забудьте провести персональную настройку сайта.
Возврат к странице Заглавная страница.
Welcome, Newnewuser!
Your account has been created. Do not forget to change your Wikipedia preferences.
Logging you in to Wikimedia's other projects: (what's this?)

Figure 5.2. Screenshot of the page received after creating a new user on Russian Wikipedia.

PERCENTAGE OF MALE AND FEMALE USERS IN DIFFERENT LANGUAGE EDITIONS OF WIKIPEDIA

The second level of analysis focuses on users who expressed their gender. In this subset, what is the percentage of male and female users (RQ2)?

The sample comprised again solely the users registered since 2010 in all language editions of Wikipedia. In this case we additionally excluded Wikipedias in which the number of users who expressed gender is less than one thousand to obtain a meaningful sample to compare the percentage of females and males, and this additional filter left forty-six language editions of Wikipedia.

Table 5.2 shows the percentage of users who indicated their gender as female. In the English Wikipedia, taken as a comparative baseline, women are 17.36 percent of the 353,056 users who expressed their gender. Respectively, 82.64 percent have indicated themselves as males. These numbers are a bit higher compared to previously conducted surveys,[24, 25] which identified 10 percent of contributors as female, but this number is still far away from the desired percentage of 25 percent expressed by Wikimedia Foundation in their strategic plan.[26]

The question that we can now focus on is if, among the forty-six language editions of Wikipedia with at least twenty thousand users registered since 2010 and at least one thousand of them setting their gender, there are editions in which the percentage of females is greater than that of males, or at least in which the gender gap is more reduced. The results are summarized in table 5.2.

As shown in table 5.2, the Slovenian Wikipedia is the one in which the gender gap is narrowest: even if males are still the majority, females account for 39.93 percent of the registered users who expressed their gender. Percentages reported in table 5.2 clearly show a pattern: nine of thirteen of the Wikipedias with relatively more females are related to languages spoken in Eastern Europe while two of them are spoken in East Asia.

Looking at the other side of the list, the Wikipedias with the smallest percentage of females are reported in table 5.3. The smallest shares of females are all present in Wikipedias in languages spoken in India that comprise Hindi, Bengali, Malayalam, Tamil, and Marathi. Then there is Persian or Farsi, spoken predominantly in Iran, preceded by Chinese, Turkish, Korean, and German.

Comparing table 5.1 with tables 5.2 and 5.3, we observe there is no definitive overlap between language editions in which many users express their gender and in

Table 5.2. Wikipedias with the Largest Percentages of Users Setting Their Gender as Female

Language (Wikipedia web address)	Percentage of females among users with gender	Number of users who expressed female as gender	Number of users who expressed their gender
Slovenian (sl.wikipedia.org)	39.93%	849	2,126
Estonian (et.wikipedia.org)	38.12%	390	1,023
Lithuanian (lt.wikipedia.org)	36.20%	640	1,768
Malay (ms.wikipedia.org)	31.27%	661	2,114
Czech (cs.wikipedia.org)	30.49%	2,159	7,082
Ukrainian (uk.wikipedia.org)	30.05%	3,296	10,969
Bulgarian (bg.wikipedia.org)	30.04%	825	2,746
Thai (th.wikipedia.org)	29.42%	2,315	7,869
Georgian (ka.wikipedia.org)	29.13%	416	1,428
Hungarian (hu.wikipedia.org)	27.72%	1,459	5,264
Catalan (ca.wikipedia.org)	26.34%	343	1,302
Portuguese (pt.wikipedia.org)	25.86%	10,214	39,499
Russian (ru.wikipedia.org)	25.67%	35,694	139,038
...			
English (en.wikipedia.org)	17.36 %	61,288	353,056

Table 5.3. Wikipedias with the Smallest Percentages of Users Setting Gender as Female

Language (Wikipedia web address)	Percentage of females among users with gender	Number of users who expressed female as gender	Number of users who expressed their gender
French (fr.wikipedia.org)	16.94%	4,103	24,225
Indonesian (id.wikipedia.org)	16.83%	3,252	19,319
Japanese (ja.wikipedia.org)	16.82%	4,278	25,428
Arabic (ar.wikipedia.org)	16.22%	4,726	29,143
Azerbaijani (az.wikipedia.org)	16.21%	285	1,758
German (de.wikipedia.org)	15.16%	5,052	33,334
Korean (ko.wikipedia.org)	13.89%	496	3,572
Turkish (tr.wikipedia.org)	13.55%	2,353	17,370
Chinese (zh.wikipedia.org)	12.74%	5,709	44,796
Persian (fa.wikipedia.org)	11.14%	1,328	11,917
Marathi (mr.wikipedia.org)	7.75%	141	1,820
Tamil (ta.wikipedia.org)	6.07%	137	2,258
Malayalam (ml.wikipedia.org)	5.34%	71	1,330
Bengali (bn.wikipedia.org)	4.09%	65	1,589
Hindi (hi.wikipedia.org)	3.75%	76	2,024

which there are more females. The Russian, Thai, and Portuguese Wikipedia editions rank high both in terms of expressing gender and females but, for example, the Turkish Wikipedia is in fifth position according to the percentage of users expressing their gender but in a low position for the percentage of women. Similarly, on the Wikipedias in Marathi, Tamil, Japanese, Chinese, and Indonesian, more users expressed their gender than on average, but the percentage of women is among the smallest. These differences might suggest diverse reasons behind the fact that users express their gender and the fact that this gender is female.

The first part of this study, referring to gender expression on Wikipedia, could be explained, as we already did, most in terms of user interface choices. On the other hand, the relative percentage of females and males inhabiting the different instances of the sociotechnical platforms call for a different explanation.

In fact, the percentage of females in different language editions of Wikipedia can be associated with many gender-related indexes published by the United Nations, United Nations Development Programme, and World Bank with regard to the participation of women in societal life. In this contribution we concentrate on a specific report published by UNESCO in 2011 about "Women in Science."[27] The report focuses on researchers, defined as "professionals engaged in the conception or creation of new knowledge, products, processes, methods and systems, as well as in the management of these projects." This is a definition we believe many Wikipedians would find suitable for themselves as well, and it presents a list of countries with the

Table 5.4. Comparison between Percentage of Women among Researchers in a Country Based on the UNESCO Report and Percentage of Users of a Language Edition of Wikipedia That Specified Their Gender as Female

Country	Percentage of female among researchers	Official language and percentage of female among users of that language edition of Wikipedia
Eastern Europe		
Georgia	52.7%	Georgian — 29.13%
Lithuania	51.4%	Lithuanian — 36.20%
Bulgaria	47.0%	Bulgarian — 30.04%
Ukraine	44.8%	Ukrainian — 30.05%
Russian Federation	41.9%	Russian — 25.67%
Estonia	41.7%	Estonian — 38.12%
Slovenia	35.1%	Slovenian — 39.93%
Hungary	33.0%	Hungarian — 27.72%
Czech Republic	28.9%	Czech — 30.49%
East Asia		
Thailand	51.2%	Thai — 29.42%
Malaysia	37.7%	Malay — 31.27%
China	32.2%	Chinese — 12.74%
Indonesia	30.6%	Indonesian — 16.83%
Korea	15.6%	Korean — 13.89%
India	14.8%	Marathi — 7.75%
		Tamil — 6.07%
		Malayalam — 5.34%
		Bengali — 4.09%
		Hindi — 3.75%
Japan	13.0%	Japanese — 16.82%
Portuguese-speaking countries		
Brazil	48.0%	Portuguese — 25.86%
Portugal	43.0%	Portuguese — 25.86%
Western Europe		
Germany	23.2%	German — 15.16%
Austria	26.4%	German — 15.16%
France	27.4%	French — 16.94%
Turkey	36.3%	Turkish — 13.55%
Iran	26.6%	Persian — 11.14%
Arabic-speaking countries		
Tunisia	47.4%	Arabic — 16.22%
Algeria	34.8%	Arabic — 16.22%
Morocco	27.6%	Arabic — 16.22%
Libya	24.8%	Arabic — 16.22%
Saudi Arabia	1.4%	Arabic — 16.22%

percentage of women among researchers, a sort of gender gap in science. Relevant data are reported in table 5.4.

Data about female researchers for some countries are missing in the UNESCO report, such as, for example, the United States and Canada.[28]

While in the previous tables about Wikipedia each line referred to a language, in table 5.4 data refer to countries, so it is necessary to keep this important difference in mind and treat comparisons with caution. In particular, the comparison between a country and the official language of that country should be taken only for explanatory reasons. Nevertheless, it is interesting to note that the two variables seem to have a linear relationship. Repeating again the caution about a comparison between countries and languages, the Pearson correlation coefficient of the two variables is 0.7 and represents a strong linear relationship (for languages spoken in India, their average was considered, and Arabic was excluded given the large variability of countries in which that language is spoken, as we comment later).

In particular, languages spoken in countries in which the science gap is more reduced mirror the languages whose Wikipedia editions show a smaller gender gap (table 5.2). This is especially true for many Eastern European countries and for Thailand. A similar point can be made for Brazil and Portugal, countries in which Portuguese is spoken.

On the other side of the spectrum, there are Western European countries such as Germany and Austria or France, whose relative language editions of Wikipedia tend to also have fewer women contributors. Similar arguments hold for Japan, Korea, Iran, China, and Turkey—all of them ranking low both on women in science and women in the relative Wikipedias. In India the share of women in science is among the smallest (14.8 percent). Analogously, the bottom five Wikipedias, in terms of proportion of women contributors, are all in fact languages spoken in India (Marathi, Tamil, Malayalam, Bengali, Hindi). Undoubtedly, we are not claiming a perfect mapping of the two data sets, especially considering the constraints in mapping languages with countries, especially for languages such as Arabic, spoken in many diverse countries, or of Malay, spoken both in Malaysia and Indonesia, and Indonesian.

CONCLUSION

This study compared gender across 285 language editions of Wikipedia. First, we analyzed the extent to which expressing gender is a diffused practice in various Wikipedias. We conclude that the differences in the amount of users expressing their gender can be explained by the differences in the interfaces, both the visibility of gender and the incentive to express it, especially during the process of the new user-profile creation.

The second research question focused on the cross-Wikipedia evaluation of the gender gap. Overall results show that there is not a single sociotechnical system in which women constitute the majority, thus confirming that the gender gap is not just present in the English Wikipedia but it is diffused across all language editions of Wikipedia. However, there are notable differences: in some Wikipedias (Slovenian, Estonian, Lithuanian) the percentage of women is close to 40 percent, but in others (Bengali, Hindi) it is around 4 percent, while on the English Wikipedia, the chosen baseline given its international nature reaches 17 percent.

Notably, languages whose editions of Wikipedia have larger shares of women tend to be spoken in countries with a larger participation of women in science. In conclusion, we observe that, even if Wikipedia is an online system, it reflects the real-world societies that inhabit the different language versions of it, and across languages and countries there are differences in women participation in public life. In particular, given that the context of Wikipedia is about creating knowledge, the best explanatory factor is the participation of women in knowledge-creation activities: the gender gap in different language editions of Wikipedia reflects the gender gap in science across the different countries of the real world.

Future research should conduct interviews with Wikipedians to identify benefits and drawbacks of visible gender settings as well as possible techniques that would encourage more diverse populations of these sociotechnical systems.

NOTES

1. Noam Cohen, "Define Gender Gap? Look up Wikipedia's Contributor List," *New York Times*, January 30, 2011, http://www.nytimes.com/2011/01/31/business/media/31link.html?_r=1&hpw.

2. Wikimedia Foundation, Editor Survey 2011, http://meta.wikimedia.org/wiki/Editor_Survey_2011.

3. Cohen, "Define Gender Gap?"

4. Wikimedia Foundation. Editor Survey 2011.

5. Paolo Massa and Federico Scrinzi, "Exploring Linguistic Points of View of Wikipedia," in *Proceedings of the 7th International Symposium on Wikis and Open Collaboration* (Mountain View, CA: ACM, 2011, 213–14).

6. Wikimedia Foundation, *Wikimedia Strategic Plan: A Collaborative Vision for the Movement through 2015*, February 2011, http://upload.wikimedia.org/wikipedia/commons/c/c0/WMF_StrategicPlan2011_spreads.pdf.

7. Judd Antin, Raymond Yee, Coye Cheshire, and Oded Nov, "Gender Differences in Wikipedia Editing," in *Proceedings of the 7th International Symposium on Wikis and Open Collaboration* (Mountain View, CA: ACM, 2011, 11–14).

8. Shyong K. Lam, Anuradha Uduwage, Zhenhua Dong, Shilad Sen, David R. Musicant, Loren Terveen, and John Riedl, "WP:Clubhouse? An Exploration of Wikipedia's Gender Imbalance," in *Proceedings of the 7th International Symposium on Wikis and Open Collaboration* (Mountain View, CA: ACM, 2011, 1–10).

9. Benjamin Collier and Julia Bear, "Conflict, Criticism, or Confidence: An Empirical Examination of the Gender Gap in Wikipedia Contributions," in *Proceedings of the ACM 2012 Conference on Computer Supported Cooperative Work* (Seattle, WA: ACM, 2012, 383–92).

10. Joseph Reagle and Lauren Rhue, "Gender Bias in Wikipedia and Britannica," *International Journal of Communication* 5 (2011). Published electronically August 8, 2011, http://ijoc.org/ojs/index.php/ijoc/article/view/777/631.

11. Noriko Hara, Pnina Shachaf, and Khe Foon Hew, "Cross-Cultural Analysis of the Wikipedia Community," *Journal of the American Society for Information Science and Technology* 61, no. 10 (2010): 2097–2108.

12. Ulrike Pfeil, Panayiotis Zaphiris, and Chee Siang Ang, "Cultural Differences in Collaborative Authoring of Wikipedia," *Journal of Computer-Mediated Communication* 12, no. 1 (2006): 88–113.

13. Sabine Niederer and José van Dijck, "Wisdom of the Crowd or Technicity of Content? Wikipedia as a Sociotechnical System," *New Media & Society* 12, no. 8 (2010): 1368–87.

14. Massa and Scrinzi, "Exploring Linguistic Points of View of Wikipedia," 213–14.

15. Our script is released as open source so that other researchers can replicate our analysis and also improve it. The Python script is at https://github.com/volpino/toolserver-scripts/blob/master/python_scripts/get_gender_table.py.

16. Brent Hecht and Darren Gergle, "The Tower of Babel Meets Web 2.0: User-Generated Content and Its Applications in a Multilingual Context," in *Proceedings of the SIGCHI Conference on Human Factors in Computing Systems* (Atlanta, GA: ACM, 2010, 291–300).

17. Wikimedia Foundation, Editor Survey 2011.

18. Cliff Lampe, Nicole Ellison, and Charles Steinfield, "A Familiar Face(Book): Profile Elements as Signals in an Online Social Network," in *Proceedings of the SIGCHI Conference on Human Factors in Computing Systems* (San Jose, CA: ACM, 2007, 435–44).

19. Kristin Stecher and Scott Counts, "Thin Slices of Online Profile Attributes," *Proceedings of ICWSM* (January 2008).

20. Paolo Massa, Maurizio Napolitano, Federico Scrinzi, and Michela Ferron, "WikiTrip: Animated Visualization over Time of Geo-Location and Gender of Wikipedians Who Edited a Page," in *Proceedings of Wikisym 2012: The International Symposium on Wikis and Open Collaboration*, Linz, Austria, 2012.

21. Wikipedia:What Wikipedia is not, http://en.wikipedia.org/wiki/Wikipedia:What_Wikipedia_is_not.

22. Sue Gardner, "Nine Reasons Women Don't Edit Wikipedia (in Their Own Words)," February 19, 2011, http://suegardner.org/2011/02/19/nine-reasons-why-women-dont-edit-wikipedia-in-their-own-words/.

23. E-mail sent by Erik Möller, deputy director of the Wikimedia Foundation, to the Gendergap MediaWiki mailing list, February 14, 2011, http://lists.wikimedia.org/pipermail/gendergap/2011-February/000449.html.

24. Cohen, "Define Gender Gap?"

25. Wikimedia Foundation, Editor Survey 2011.

26. Wikimedia Foundation, *Wikimedia Strategic Plan.*

27. UNESCO, "Women in Science by Region, Female Researchers in 2009," http://www.uis.unesco.org/FactSheets/Documents/fs14-women-science-2011-en.pdf.

28. UNESCO, "Women in Science by Region, Female Researchers in 2009."

6

Knowledge Sharing on Wikimedia Embassies

Pnina Fichman and Noriko Hara

INTRODUCTION

With the proliferation of the social web, online knowledge sharing across cultural boundaries has become a norm. For example, the English Wikipedia attracts users from all over the world, and much of Wikipedia is written in languages other than English. Intercultural collaboration occurs daily on Wikipedia with users from all over the world making valued contributions. Online intercultural collaboration on Wikipedia is intriguing but understudied, as the majority of research on Wikipedia is based on the English site with few exceptions. Existing cross-cultural research on Wikipedia includes comparative accounts of Wikipedia in multiple languages (e.g., Callahan and Herring 2011; Hara, Shachaf, and Hew 2010; Pfeil, Zaphiris, and Ang 2006; Stvilia, Al-Faraj, and Yi 2009) and case studies of Wikipedia in languages other than English (e.g., Han-Teng 2009; Shachaf and Hara 2010). More scholarly attention is needed in order to understand the ways in which the social web can mediate, facilitate, or hinder intercultural collaboration and how this, in turn, can influence knowledge sharing.

The chapter aims to address this gap by identifying the style of interaction that characterizes global knowledge-sharing behaviors on Wikipedia as well as the topics that are posted by users from various countries on Wikimedia Embassies, which assist in cross-lingual projects. More broadly, the research we present here emphasizes a sociotechnical understanding of Wikipedia, and it is particularly informed by social informatics. Social informatics is "the interdisciplinary study of the design, uses, and consequences of Information and Communication Technologies (ICTs) that takes into account their interaction with institutional and cultural contexts" (Kling, Rosenbaum, and Sawyer 2005, 6). As such, it illustrates the ways in which technology facilitates and mediates intercultural collaboration in an international context, and seeks to answer the question: How do users with diverse national and linguistic backgrounds engage in global, boundary-spanning activities online? The study also delineates how the technological infrastructure is appropriated for local and global use, and how activities on Wikimedia Embassies can enhance our understanding of Wikipedia at the local and global level. Wikimedia Embassies offer useful insights into how cultural and institutional contexts interact with each other and how such contexts influence online knowledge sharing.

BACKGROUND

Knowledge Sharing in a Multicultural and Global Setting

One of the most active online activities in recent years is knowledge sharing (e.g., Qualman 2011). Due to the widespread use of the social web and the Internet in general, people from different countries participate in knowledge-sharing activities both as parts of organizations and individually. Scholars are intrigued by this phenomenon and are committed to investigating knowledge sharing in multicultural environments, although they have displayed varying levels of sensitivity to the cross-cultural factors that affect knowledge sharing. For example, previous studies that focused on knowledge sharing in corporate multicultural settings have criticized the prominent knowledge management model that was developed by Nonaka and Takeuchi (1995), which was adopted in many countries and especially in the United States (Weir and Hutchings 2005). Weir and Hutchings contended that because the original model was appropriated in Japan—within a specific cultural context—its application in other countries needed to be used cautiously, but that some aspects of the model were actually applicable to China and the Arab world, and they emphasized a culturally sensitive approach to knowledge-sharing practices. Other scholars have called for more research on online knowledge sharing in multicultural settings (Ardichvili et al. 2006), while some have investigated how national culture influences knowledge-sharing practices in online environments (Li 2010; Qiu, Lin, and Leung 2013; Siau, Erickson, and Nah 2010; Zhang, de Pablos, and Xu 2013).

Ardichvili et al. (2006) studied cultural influences on online knowledge sharing at Caterpillar, a multinational corporation. The online communities of practice they examined involved interviewees from China, Russia, Brazil, and the United States. Their findings indicate that an individual's cultural influence with respect to knowledge-sharing practices is less apparent than expected, contending that an individual's national culture is less influential than Caterpillar corporate culture, and they in turn call for further examination of cross-cultural knowledge-sharing practices in smaller multinational companies.

Li (2010) interviewed participants from China and the United States in order to identify factors that affect online knowledge-sharing behaviors in a multicultural corporate setting. She then categorized these factors into three areas: organizational issues (i.e., organizational culture, work practice, and performance expectancy), national cultural differences (i.e., language, different logic, and difference in perceived credibility of shared knowledge), and nature of online communities of practice (i.e., advantages of easily sharing knowledge and archival capabilities, disadvantages of discussing sensitive issues, and competition with other media channels). As in previous research, Li (2010) emphasized the importance of organizational support for online knowledge sharing, yet she also identified the other two areas that affect online knowledge sharing: national cultural differences and the nature of online communities of practices.

Zhang, de Pablos, and Xu (2013) found that cultural values affect knowledge-sharing behaviors in a multinational virtual classroom with students from China, Hong Kong, and the Netherlands. Students from highly collectivistic cultures (China and Hong Kong) shared more information than the students from the less collectivistic culture (the Netherlands). They found that "saving face" both positively and negatively affected online knowledge-sharing behaviors. This finding was not in line with the Ardichvili et al. (2006) study, in which saving face was not an issue. Zhang et al. suggested studying more countries and interactions over longer periods of time.

Focusing on cultural differences on social networking sites, Qiu, Lin, and Leung (2013) examined the difference between two social networking sites: Facebook (American) and Renren (Chinese) in terms of students' in-group sharing behaviors (e.g., sharing links). They found that participants in Renren engaged more in sharing behaviors than the same participants on Facebook. They concluded that Renren users are more influenced by a collectivistic culture, yet the same users can switch and adopt to the expected culture of Facebook.

Siau, Erickson, and Nah (2010) examined eighteen online communities from Yahoo! Groups to find Americans and Chinese that exist outside organizations. They argued that the traits they found in these online communities reflect national cultures identified along the following Hofstede dimensions: power, distance, and individuals-collectivism (Hofstede 1980; Hofstede, van Hofstede, and Minkov 1991). Siau, Erickson, and Nah (2010) concluded that national cultures significantly influence knowledge-sharing tendencies in open online communities.

It is imperative to examine both intercultural collaboration in general and online knowledge sharing in multicultural settings in particular, because 1) social media has become prevalent in many countries, facilitating knowledge-sharing globally (e.g., Qiu, Lin, and Leung 2013); 2) many multinational organizations require employees to work in global virtual teams (e.g., Zakaria, Amelinckx, and Wilemon 2004); 3) existing studies examine cultural influences on knowledge-sharing behaviors but generally do not pay attention to the content of knowledge sharing in multicultural environments; and, above all, 4) there is a need to understand multicultural knowledge-sharing practices that occur outside traditional organizational boundaries, as most of the existing studies are confined to the context of traditional organizational settings.

Using social informatics lenses, this chapter argues that insights from one context should not be extrapolated as is to another context. The chapter is premised on the assumption that context matters and therefore pays attention to the unique processes that bridge various institutional and cultural contexts in Wikipedia.

Global Wikipedia

Scholars that study how cultures influence online interaction in the context of Wikipedia have also investigated the variations across different Wikipedia language versions. Most comparative cross-cultural studies of Wikipedia in multiple languages have included a convenient sample of languages and have grounded their analysis and interpretations in Hofstede's dimensions of cultural diversity (e.g., Callahan and Herring 2011; Hara, Shachaf, and Hew 2010; Pfeil, Zaphiris, and Ang 2006; Stvilia, Al-Faraj, and Yi 2009). For example, Callahan and Herring (2011) compared articles about prominent individuals in the Polish and English editions of Wikipedia and found that content and perspectives vary across language versions. These differences are influenced by the cultures, histories, and values of the respective countries. In another comparative study, Hara, Shachaf, and Hew (2010) conducted a cross-cultural analysis of four Wikipedia communities in different languages (English, Hebrew, Japanese, and Malay). They identified similarities and differences in behavior across the languages on the Talk, Wikipedia Talk, and User Talk pages, and they used Hofstede's framework to explain these variations. Similarly, Pfiel, Zaphiris, and Ang (2006) examined the relationship between national culture and computer-mediated communication (CMC) in four Wikipedias (French, German, Japanese, and Dutch), focusing on the entry of "game." They reported correlations between patterns of contributions and Hofstede's dimensions, suggesting that cultural differences observed in the physical world also exist in the virtual world. These studies provide evidence for the existence of cultural and online interaction differences across the many language versions of Wikipedia, much of it in line with and supporting Hofstede's framework.

Another type of research on Wikipedia that goes beyond the English Wikipedia involves case studies in other languages. These intracultural studies typically research an aspect of online collaboration in their respective Wikipedia communities; two such examples have been conducted in the Chinese and Hebrew Wikipedia communities (e.g., Han-Teng 2009; Shachaf and Hara 2010; Zhang and Zhu 2011). Shachaf and Hara (2010), for example, studied troll behavior and motivation on Hebrew Wikipedia and found that trolling consists of repetitive, intentional, isolated harmful actions involving disguised virtual identities that both violate Wikipedia policies and are a destructive form of community participation. Han-Teng (2009) focused on the early stages of development of the Chinese Wikipedia and argued that, beyond technical and linguistic issues, the community must develop editorial and administrative policies and guidelines to succeed. Zhang and Zhu (2011) reported that contributors decreased their contributions by 42.8 percent on average as a result of a temporary decrease in the size of online groups (the Chinese government blocked access to Wikipedia in Mainland China during that period). These authors claim that individuals received greater social benefit when their contributions were higher in number and group sizes larger, and lesser social benefit when their contributions were fewer and their group sizes smaller.

Despite the global nature of Wikipedia, relatively little scholarly attention has been given to the cross-cultural processes of knowledge sharing on Wikipedia in particular and on the social web in general. In addition to the other chapters in this book that address this particular gap, this chapter also attempts to offer insight into the style and content of knowledge sharing among participants from different countries, based on an analysis of a sample of twenty-one Wikimedia Embassy Talk pages.

METHOD

Setting

We chose to collect data regarding knowledge sharing and intercultural collaboration on Wikipedia from discussion pages (called "Talk pages") of various Wikimedia Embassies. Wikimedia is an overarching nonprofit organization that operates behind Wikipedia and supports other projects such as Wikibooks and Wikidata. Its mission is to share free educational content through various projects around the world (http://www.wikimedia.org/). Wikimedia Embassy[1] was established to provide support for cross language projects and interlanguage issues. The first entry on the Wikimedia Embassy page was made on November 15, 2003, and as of July 28, 2013, there were Wikimedia Embassies in 123 languages. Each Wikimedia Embassy lists ambassadors who can help with specific languages.

Data Collection

We sampled thirty-four of the existing Wikimedia Embassies in July 2011 and coded a total of 276 posts in English from twenty-one Talk pages. Thirteen out of the thirty-four Embassies that had inactive links, no discussions, or no discussions in English were thereby excluded from analysis. We coded the following Wikipedia Embassy Talk pages: Afrikaans, Armenian, Bishnupriya Manipuri, Classical Chinese, Croatian, Danish, Dutch, Esperanto, French, German, Greek, Interlingua, Korean, Latin, Low Saxon, Malay, Occitan, Russian, Spanish, Ukranian, and Waray-Waray (appendix A).

Data Analysis

Similar to previous studies (e.g., Hara, Shachaf, and Hew 2010), we developed an original inductive coding scheme based on the data of two active Wikimedia Embassies: English and German. These two Embassies were chosen because they were the two most active Wikipedias. We then tested and modified the coding scheme on the Dutch and Russian Wikimedia Embassies to validate our scheme. The final coding scheme is presented in appendix B. To facilitate coding we used NVivo 8—software designed for qualitative data analysis. We coded individual posts as the unit of analysis and calculated percentages of codes for the entire data set and per Embassy.

Limitations

Although some posts on the various Wikimedia Embassies were not written in English, we restricted our analysis only to English posts, because we are not fluent in all twenty-one languages. This means that this chapter provides only a partial account of the interactions that occur on Wikimedia Embassies, because non-English posts could differ significantly in style and content from English posts.

FINDINGS AND DISCUSSION

Based on the analysis of the 276 English posts on twenty-one Wikimedia Embassies Talk pages, we identified 1) the style of interaction that characterizes knowledge-sharing behaviors and 2) the topics that are posted by users.

Style of Intercultural Interaction on Wikimedia Embassies

First, we examined the common style of intercultural communication on the Wikimedia Embassies pages. In table 6.1 we report frequencies and percentages per category and per code. Findings show that almost all of the posts are characterized by a polite communication style, which includes greetings, closings, and posts in which users introduce themselves by name. It is possible that the polite style is due to the title of the space, "Wikimedia Embassy," which connotes real-world embassies, triggering a formal and polite communication style. We found the style for intercultural communication on Wikimedia Embassies to be slightly more formal than expected, compared to the study by Hara, Shachaf, and Hew (2010), which reports that posts on Eastern Wikipedias in Japanese and Malay were more polite than posts on Western Wikipedias in English and Hebrew. Our findings indicate that politeness extends to English posts on a number of Wikimedia Embassies, which resembles a formal, direct, and polite style that allows for successful intercultural communication among heterogeneous global teams in the workplace (Shachaf 2008). Other possible explanations are that this politeness resembles the way corporate cultures have had a stronger influence on online knowledge-sharing behaviors than national cultures (Ardichvili et al. 2006), or that most users who post on Wikimedia Embassies simply imitate the style of previous posts on these Talk pages. Users are able to adopt their behaviors based on site-specific norms, in line with Qiu, Lin, and Leung (2013) findings that Chinese users were able to adapt their knowledge-sharing behaviors based on the expectations for an American platform, for example, Facebook. Likewise, a formal communication style appears to be expected on Wikimedia Embassies, making it appear that the Wikimedia Embassies' platform has a stronger influence on online interaction behaviors than an individual's national culture.

The formal style of intercultural verbal communication found on Wikimedia Embassies is referred to by Gudykunst and Ting-Toomey (1998) as the "contextual style." It encompasses a formality that reflects the social and organizational differences between people and maintains social context. The contextual style tends to be associated with high–"power distance"[2] and "high-context"[3] cultures (Gudykunst and Ting-Toomey 1998). However, because the posts are in English one could expect that the "personal style" will dominate; the personal style assumes similarity and equality and is associated with low–"power distance" and "low-context" cultures (i.e., in Western English-speaking countries). In addition, the formality of communication, as a form of respect, may be attributed to settings in which strangers interact with each other, because when people interact with strangers, one of the required conditions for effective communication is to be respectful (e.g., Ruben 1976, as cited in Gudykunst and Kim 2002). Based on our findings one wonders if the contextual style is more common online in general or only on Wikimedia Embassies. While Shachaf (2005) suggests that the formal style also enhances intercultural collaboration among heterogeneous members of global virtual teams, more research is needed to support and explain this argument.

Furthermore, in cross-cultural research, politeness has been associated with high–power distance culture and high-context cultures. On Wikipedia, politeness was also identified in Eastern Wikipedias and Wikipedias that contain over a million articles (Hara, Shachaf, and Hew 2010). It is interesting to note that similar to the results in Hara, Shachaf, and Hew's (2010) study, we found that Eastern Wikimedia Embassies have more frequent posts that indicate a polite communication style than Western Wikimedia Embassies (table 6.2). For instance, the Classical Chinese Embassy shows one of the two highest percentages of politeness codes among all embassies (77.78 percent) (table 6.2).

Table 6.1. Style of Posts

Code Name		Embassies (N = 21); number of Embassies and percentages of embassies out of 21	Codes (N = 276); number of posts and percentages out of 276
Style	Closings	20 (95.2%)	213 (77.17%)
	Greetings	21 (100.0%)	167 (60.51%)
	Introducing oneself by name	17 (80.9%)	38 (13.77%)

Note: The percentages for Embassies were calculated by dividing the number of Embassies for a specific category by the total number of Embassies (i.e., N= 21). The percentages for codes were calculated by dividing the number of codes for a specific category by the total number of posts (i.e., N = 276).

Table 6.2. Style of Posts in Twenty-One Wikimedia Embassies

	Closings—number of posts and percentages out of total number of English posts	Greetings—number of posts and percentages out of total number of English posts	Introducing oneself by name—number of posts and percentages out of total number of English posts	Total number of English posts	Total percentage of communication style codes
Afrikaans Embassy	10 (100.00%)	6 (60.00%)	2 (20.00%)	10	60.00%
Armenian Embassy	13 (92.86%)	13 (92.86%)	3 (21.43%)	14	69.05%
Bishnupriya Manipuri Embassy	25 (64.10%)	8 (20.51%)	2 (5.12%)	15	29.91%
Classical Chinese Embassy	2 (66.67%)	3 (100.00%)	2 (66.67%)	3	77.78%
Croatian Embassy	6 (85.71%)	6 (85.71%)	0	7	57.14%
Danish Embassy	1 (50.00%)	1 (50.00%)	0	2	33.33%
Dutch Embassy	23 (85.19%)	20 (74.07%)	4 (14.81%)	27	58.02%
Esperanto Embassy	2 (33.33%)	4 (66.67%)	3 (50.00%)	6	50.00%
French Embassy	5 (83.33%)	4 (66.67%)	1 (16.67%)	6	55.56%
German Embassy	18 (54.55%)	16 (48.48%)	1 (3.03%)	33	35.35%
Greek Embassy	16 (61.54%)	17 (65.38%)	4 (15.38%)	26	47.44%
Interlingua Embassy	1 (100.00%)	1 (100.00%)	1 (100.00%)	1	100.00%
Korean Embassy	9 (100.00%)	7 (77.78%)	2 (22.22%)	9	66.67%
Latin Embassy	5 (26.32%)	7 (36.84%)	3 (15.79%)	19	26.32%
Low Saxon Embassy	0	1 (100.00%)	1 (100.00%)	1	66.67%
Malay Embassy	4 (80.00%)	2 (40.00%)	0	5	40.00%
Occitan Embassy	1 (100.00%)	1 (100.00%)	0	1	66.67%
Russian Embassy	46 (79.31%)	27 (46.55%)	4 (6.90%)	58	44.25%
Spanish Embassy	8 (88.89%)	7 (77.78%)	1 (11.11%)	9	59.26%
Ukranian Embassy	15 (75.00%)	12 (60.00%)	2 (10.00%)	20	48.33%
Waray-Waray Embassy	3 (75.00%)	4 (100.00%)	2 (50.00%)	4	75.00%

Note: The total percentages of communication style codes were calculated by dividing the total numbers of all three style codes (i.e., greetings, closing, and introducing oneself by name) by the total number of English posts times three.

Content of Intercultural Interaction on Wikimedia Embassies

In addition to the style, we classified knowledge-sharing activities under the following three content categories: 1) content management, a category of postings about the content of Wikipedia articles as well as other Wikipedia policy pages or Wikipedia projects pages; 2) international context, a category of translations, international entries, and the coordination of efforts against copyright violation and vandalism; and 3) collaboration, a category of cross language coordination efforts inside and outside Wikipedia. We report frequencies and percentages for each of the codes organized in the above categories (table 6.3). The percentages were calculated against the total number of posts in English. We also provide examples of posts to illustrate each category.

1) Content management: Over 80 percent of the Embassies include posts about Wikipedia content. One of the most frequent requests for action in this category involves requests to adjust user names across Wikipedias in multiple languages. For instance, a typical post looks like this: "Is it possible (as on French WP) to rename my account? I'd like it to be Gebruiker:TwoWings instead. Thank you to answer on

Table 6.3.   Content of Posts

Code Name		Embassies (N = 21); number of Embassies and percentages out of 21 Embassies	Codes (N = 276); number of posts and percentages out of 276 English posts
1) Content Management	Wikipedia— Action	17 (80.9%)	140 (50.72%)
	Wikipedia— Information	18 (85.7%)	66 (23.91%)
2) International Context	International Entries	6 (28.5%)	7 (2.54%)
	Terminology	5 (23.8%)	25 (9.06%)
	Translation	17 (80.9%)	132 (47.83%)
	Vandalism— Copyright Violations— Blocking Users	8 (38.0%)	24 (8.70%)
3) Collaboration	External Cross Language Project	11 (52.3%)	21 (7.61%)
	Internal Cross Language Project	13 (61.9%)	21 (7.61%)

Note: The percentages for Embassies were calculated by dividing the number of Embassies for a specific category by the total number of Embassies (N = 21). The percentages for codes were calculated by dividing the number of codes for a specific category by the total number of posts (N = 276).

my page." These requests become popular as users become active in more than one language Wikipedia and want to unify their user names across multiple Wikipedias. This activity facilitates global collaboration across Wikipedia languages, as individual users can easily act on multiple Wikipedias using the same user name and behave as "boundary spanners" across various Wikipedia language versions (Hara and Fichman 2014). Boundary spanners are the users who aim to contribute to multiple Wikipedia projects and interact on various Wikimedia Embassies, asking and responding to requests for globalized user names. When Wikipedia's global users post and respond to these requests, they develop the basic infrastructure that supports cross language activities. These content management activities contribute to "knowledge shaping" (Yates, Wagner, and Majchrzak 2010). Yates, Wagner, and Majchrzak argue the importance of knowledge shaping, which deals with editing and restructuring the content of Wiki entries. Although these activities, like helping users obtain universal usernames, are not visible and do not get much credit as knowledge contribution, they are crucial to assisting in knowledge sharing.

Wikimedia Embassies play a major role in these types of requests and provide a platform for information exchange. In this way the Wikipedia infrastructure, as well as existing global and local policies about user names, enable boundary-spanning activity. Boundary objects are shared objects that facilitate the bridging of different groups (of each language version of Wikipedia) and assist in the intersecting of different communities on Wikimedia Embassies. Wikipedia's policies, organizational structure, and projects serve as boundary objects that provide the foundations for online collaboration on this mass content production. As such, Wikimedia Embassies are a manifestation of boundary objects.

2) International context: As expected, knowledge-sharing activities on the Wikimedia Embassy pages involve many posts that have international contexts. Found on most Embassy pages (80.9 percent), this category includes numerous requests for translation. More interestingly, over one-third of the Embassies include postings about acts of vandalism, which primarily discuss copyright violations and blocking users who are active in multiple Wikipedias. Many vandals, like other users, participate in numerous Wikipedias and can cause damage throughout multiple languages when efforts to block them are not coordinated. It is useful to restrain certain users simultaneously on various Wikipedias, because a malicious user may be blocked on the English Wikipedia, for example, while she or he can still be active in causing trouble on the German, French, and Spanish Wikipedias. Coordinating efforts to block these users save Wikipedia administrators time and effort; in fact, fighting vandals is one of their major tasks (Riehle 2006). While it is unclear if and how Wikipedia vandals coordinate (Shachaf and Hara 2010) and act globally, Wikipedia administrators coordinate efforts to fight against the global spread of vandalism.

Other common posts in this category were related to copyright violations. Perhaps it is a common issue for global Wikipedians, as the understanding of copyright differs in various countries (Shachaf and Rubenstein 2007). For example, the following comment was posted in the Afrikaans Embassy:

People in English Wikipedia have found out that the image doesn't belong to the public domain. Instead, you can only use it for non-commercial or educational purposes. Such is too restrictive licence [license] for Wikipedia. [1] You can't even use the image in Wikipedia under United States copyright law. In English Wikipedia they are going to delete the image. I think that you should do the same because the Wikipedia servers are located in United States.

Wikipedia administrators on the Wikimedia Embassies page pay attention to violations of copyright based on U.S. laws and need to negotiate about the acts of users who come from countries with different conceptualizations of copyright. The Licensing Policy page of Wikimedia states, "All projects are expected to host only content which is under a Free Content License, or which is otherwise free as recognized by the 'Definition of Free Cultural Works,'"[4] which is defined as "works or expressions which can be freely studied, applied, copied and/or modified, by anyone, for any purpose."[5] Because some countries have less strict understandings of copyright, violations of copyright in one country cannot be interpreted at face value as such in another country. The concept of copyright and ownership manifests itself also in online behaviors of individuals, groups, and even local institutions, such as libraries (Shachaf and Rubenstein 2007). From a cultural point of view, even if all users operated under the same laws, individuals from different countries still would approach rules and regulations in different ways. In particularistic cultures the law is only a point of departure, and adherence to rules and regulation is context dependent, whereas in other cultures, for example, universalistic ones, individuals put high importance on observing the laws (Trompenaars and Hampden-Turner 1998).

3) Collaboration: One of the goals of Wikimedia Embassies is to facilitate collaboration on cross language issues, yet, contrary to our expectations, little has been posted on Wikipedia Embassies Talk pages explicitly about (internal or external) cross language projects; these posts appeared on only half of the Wikimedia Embassies. For example, a user discusses Wikizine, a wiki newsletter for global use by Wikipedia users across multiple language versions:

> You know it is not easy for the members of a local wiki to be informed about what is going on in the higher levels of the Wikimedia family. This [is] because of the language problem and the high level of fragmentation of places where you can find information.
>
> I am now making a weekly newsletter (Wikizine) that attempts to provide the news of the Wikimedia projects. . . . I can only create one version in something that [is] supposed to be English. I count on the readers to inform there [their] local wiki about the news in there [their] own language. . . .
>
> I hope that you can [and] others of your wiki will subscribe to Wikizine and give feedback. So that Wikizine can become really a source where Wikimedians can find out what is going on.

It is possible that because Wikimedia Embassies are not very visible for most Wikipedia users, much of this type of coordination happens on the Talk pages of individual Wikipedia administrators. Further examination of users' Talk pages may support this potential explanation. With more than 280 language versions of Wikipedia, it may become more important to facilitate cross language projects in the future, and Wikimedia Embassies have the potential to facilitate such projects.

We can conclude that many of the posts on Wikimedia Embassies deal with requests for translations, change of user names, copyright violations, and vandalism. Wikimedia Embassies thus serve an important platform, perhaps one of many, which facilitate intercultural collaboration on the social web, enabling online boundary crossing between users from different Wikipedia language versions. This study exemplifies how boundary spanners (e.g., vandals, administrators) work and how boundary objects such as Wikizine serve to support online knowledge sharing in cross-cultural environments.

CONCLUSIONS

One dimension of the social web is its potential to facilitate global collaboration, yet knowledge sharing through intercultural interactions and global collaboration has rarely been the focus of previous scholarly works. This chapter provides insight into these processes, examining knowledge-sharing activities on Wikimedia Embassies. We analyzed the data for communication style and knowledge-sharing content. Findings indicated that intercultural communication style tends to be polite, perhaps because it is natural to use formal communication style when communicating in English with strangers from other countries (Gudykunst and Kim 2002). Future research should aim to identify effective intercultural communication styles and successful collaborations to support online knowledge sharing among users from various countries. For example, the following research questions can be pursued: Do similar communication styles apply in face-to-face contexts, organizational online communities, and online communities, or do these styles differ based on context? To what extent does the social web facilitate or hinder boundary spanning when language barriers are involved?

Our study shows that traces of contextual differences in communication style exist between online and offline intercultural communication. These findings are in line with prior research in organizational settings (Shachaf 2008). Additionally, we analyzed the content of posts using the following three categories: 1) content management, 2) international context, and 3) collaboration. Findings show that the most frequently posted messages include 1) requests for translation in order to overcome language barriers, 2) requests to allow users to work across language boundaries with the same user name and thereby serve as boundary spanners, and 3) collaboration efforts to fight against vandalism and copyright violation on a global scale.

Finally, from a sociotechnical point of view this study presents how both Wikipedia users and the Wikipedia infrastructure allow for and trigger these types of interactions and how contextual cultural variations can be standardized on the global Wikipedia. More broadly, this study contributes to the domain of social informatics.

Studies in social informatics emphasize the importance of contexts (Kling, Rosenbaum, and Sawyer 2005). This study sheds light on the mechanisms of knowledge sharing in a particular context: cross-cultural knowledge sharing in a Web 2.0 environment. Future research should aim at examining 1) processes of boundary crossing as well as types and properties of boundaries and boundary spanners on Wikipedia in particular (Hara and Fichman 2014) and the social web in general, and 2) intercultural collaboration on global collaborative projects.

NOTES

1. For more information on the Wikimedia Embassy, see http://meta.wikimedia.org/wiki/Wikipedia_Embassy.

2. *Power distance* refers to the distance among different people in different levels of the hierarchy. It is "the extent to which the less powerful members of institutions and organizations within a country expect and accept that power is distributed unequally" (Hofstede, van Hofstede, and Minkov 1991, 28).

3. Communication in a culture takes place in a context. In low-context cultures, the message is expressed with no assumptions that there is shared knowledge in the context. Nothing is left for the receiver of the message to interpret, and no information is assumed to be there in the first place. In high-context culture, the context bears a lot of the information that helps the receiver to decode the message; there are limited words that will be pronounced, and a lot is assumed to be known already, so there is no need to repeat the message. In a high-context culture, there is a distinct difference between in-group and out-group members, whereas in the low context, a group's boundaries are more permeable.

4. Resolution:Licensing policy, http://wikimediafoundation.org/wiki/Resolution:Licensing_policy.

5. Definition of Free Cultural Works, FreedomDefined.org, http://freedomdefined.org/Definition.

REFERENCES

Ardichvili, Alexandre, Martin Maurer, Wei Li, Tim Wentling, and Reed Stuedemann. 2006. "Cultural Influences on Knowledge Sharing through Online Communities of Practice." *Journal of Knowledge Management* 10, no. 1 (2006): 94–107.

Callahan, Ewa S., and Susan C. Herring. 2011. "Cultural Bias in Wikipedia Articles about Famous Persons." *Journal of the American Society for Information Science and Technology* 62, no. 10: 1899–1915. doi: 10.1002/asi.

Gudykunst, William B., and Young Yun Kim. 2002. *Communicating with Strangers: An Approach to Intercultural Communication*, 4th edition. New York: McGraw-Hill Higher Education, 2002.

Gudykunst, William B., and Stella Ting-Toomey. 1988. *Culture and Interpersonal Communication*. Newbury Park, CA: Sage.

Han-Teng, Liao. 2009. "Conflict and Consensus in the Chinese Version of Wikipedia." *IEEE Technology and Society Magazine* 28, no. 2.

Hara, Noriko, and Pnina Fichman. 2014. "Frameworks for Understanding Knowledge Sharing in Open Online Communities: Boundaries and Boundary Crossing." In *Social Informatics: Past, Present and Future*, edited by P. Fichman and H. Rosenbaum. Newcastle, UK: Cambridge Scholars Publishing.

Hara, Noriko, Pnina Shachaf, and Khe Foon Hew. 2010. "Cross-Cultural Analysis of Wikipedia Community." *Journal of the American Society of Information Science and Technology* 61, no. 10: 2097–2108.

Hofstede, Geert. 1980. *Culture's Consequences: International Differences in Work-Related Values*. Beverly Hills, CA: Sage.

Hofstede, Geert, Gert van Hofstede, and Michael Minkov. 1991. *Cultures and Organizations: Software of the Mind*. London: McGraw-Hill.

Kling, Rob, Howard Rosenbaum, and Steve Sawyer. 2005. "Understanding and Communicating Social Informatics: A Framework for Studying and Teaching the Human Contexts of Information and Communication Technologies." Medford, NJ: Information Today, Inc..

Li, Wei. 2010. "Virtual Knowledge Sharing in a Cross-Cultural Context." *Journal of Knowledge Management* 14, no. 1: 38–50.

Nonaka, Ikujiro, and Hirotaka Takeuchi. 1995. *The Knowledge-Creating Company: How Japanese Companies Create the Dynamics of Innovation*. New York: Oxford University Press.

Pfeil, Ulrike, Panayiotis Zaphiris, and Chee Siang Ang. 2006. "Cultural Differences in Collaborative Authoring of Wikipedia." *Journal of Computer-Mediated Communication* 12, no. 1, article 5. http://jcmc.indiana.edu/vol12/issue1/pfeil.html.

Qualman, Erik. 2011. *Socialnomics: How Social Media Transforms the Way We Live and Do Business*. Hoboken, NJ: Wiley.

Qiu, Lin, Han Lin, and Angela K.-y. Leung. 2013. "Cultural Differences and Switching of In-Group Sharing Behavior between an American (Facebook) and a Chinese (Renren) Social Networking Site." *Journal of Cross-Cultural Psychology* 44, no. 1: 106–21.

Riehle, Dirk. 2006. "How and Why Wikipedia Works: An Interview with Angela Beesley, Elisabeth Bauer, and Kizu Naoko." *WikiSym '06*, August 21–23, 2006, Odense, Denmark. http://www.riehle.org/computer-science/research/2006/wikisym-2006-interview.pdf.

Setlock, Leslie D., and Susan Fussell. 2011. "Culture or Fluency? Unpacking Interactions between Culture and Communication Medium." *CHI 2011*, Vancouver, BC, Canada.

Shachaf, Pnina. 2005. "Bridging Cultural Diversity through Email." *Journal of Global Information Technology Management* 8, no. 2: 46–60.

Shachaf, Pnina. 2008. "Cultural Diversity and Information and Communication Technology Impacts on Global Virtual Teams: An Exploratory Study." *Information and Management* 45, no. 2: 131–42.

Shachaf, Pnina, and Noriko Hara. 2010. "Beyond Vandalism: Wikipedia Trolls." *Journal of Information Science* 36, no. 3.

Shachaf, Pnina, and Ellen Rubenstein. 2007. "A Comparative Analysis of Libraries' Approaches to Copyright: Israel, Russia, and the U.S." *Journal of Academic Librarianship* 33, no. 1: 94–105.

Siau, K., J. Erickson, and F. F. H. Nah. 2010. "Effects of National Culture on Types of Knowledge Sharing in Virtual Communities." *IEEE Transactions on Professional Communication* 53, no. 3: 278–92.

Stvilia, Besiki, Abdullah Al-Faraj, and Yong Jeong Yi. 2009. "Issues of Cross-Contextual Information Quality Evaluation—the Case of Arabic, English, and Korean Wikipedias." *Library & Information Science Research* 31, no. 4: 232–39.

Trompenaars, Fons, and Charles Hampden-Turner. 1998. *Riding the Waves of Culture: Understanding Cultural Diversity in Business.* New York: McGraw-Hill.

Weir, David, and Kate Hutchings. 2005. "Cultural Embeddedness and Contextual Constraints: Knowledge Sharing in Chinese and Arab Cultures." *Knowledge and Process Management* 12, no. 2: 89–98. doi: 10.1002/kpm.222.

Yates, Dave, Christian Wagner, and Ann Majchrzak. 2010. "Factors Affecting Shapers of Organizational Wikis." *Journal of the American Society for Information Science and Technology* 61, no. 3: 543–54.

Zakaria, Norhayati, Andrea Amelinckx, and David Wilemon. 2004. "Working Together Apart? Building a Knowledge-Sharing Culture for Global Virtual Teams." *Creativity and Innovation Management* 13, no. 1: 15–29.

Zhang, Xi, Patricia Ordonez de Pablos, and Qingkun Xu. 2013. "Culture Effects on the Knowledge Sharing in Multi-National Virtual Classes: A Mixed Method." *Computers in Human Behavior* 31. http://dx.doi.org/10.1016/j.chb.2013.04.021.

Zhang, Xiaoquan, and Feng Zhu. 2011. "Group Size and Incentives to Contribute: A Natural Experiment at Chinese Wikipedia." *American Economic Review* 101, no. 4: 1601–15.

APPENDIX A: WIKIPEDIA EMBASSIES SAMPLE

Table 6.4.

Wikimedia Embassy Name	Number of English Posts	Embassy URL
af: Afrikaans Ambassade [Afrikaans]	10	http://af.wikipedia.org/wiki/Wikipedia:Ambassade
hy: Armenian Embassy-Հայկական Դեսպանատուն [Armenian]	14	http://hy.wikipedia.org/wiki/%D5%8E%D5%AB%D6%84%D5%AB%D5%BA%D5%A5%D5%A4%D5%AB%D5%A1:%D4%B4%D5%A5%D5%BD%D5%BA%D5%A1%D5%B6%D5%A1%D5%BF%D5%B8%D6%82%D5%B6
bpy: Bishnupriya Manipuri ইমার ঠাবর পুলবাস [Bishnupriya Manipuri]	15	http://bpy.wikipedia.org/wiki/উইকিপেডিযা:পুলবাস
zh-classical: 大使館 [Classical Chinese]	3w	http://zh-classical.wikipedia.org/wiki/%E7%B6%AD%E5%9F%BA%E5%A4%E7%E5%85%B8:%E5%A4%A7%E4%BD%BF%E9%A4%A8
hr: Hrvatsko veleposlanstvo [Croatian]	7	http://hr.wikipedia.org/wiki/Wikipedija:Veleposlanstvo
da: Dansk Ambassade (Danish Wikipedia)	2	http://da.wikipedia.org/wiki/Wikipedia:Ambassaden
nl: Ambassade (Dutch Embassy)	27	http://nl.wikipedia.org/wiki/Wikipedia:Ambassade
eo: Esperanto Ambasadorejo [Esperanto]	6	http://eo.wikipedia.org/wiki/Vikipedio:Ambasadorejo
fr: Français—Ambassade [French]	6	http://fr.wikipedia.org/wiki/Wikipédia:Ambassade
de: Deutsche Botschaft [German]	33	http://de.wikipedia.org/wiki/Wikipedia:Botschaft
el: Greek Embassy [Greek]	26	http://el.wikipedia.org/wiki/Βικιπαίδεια:Πρεσβεία
ia: Interlingua Ambassada [Interlingua]	1	http://ia.wikipedia.org/wiki/Wikipedia:Ambassada
ko: Korean Embassy [Korean]	9	http://ko.wikipedia.org/wiki/위키백과:대사관
la: Legatio [Latin]	19	http://la.wikipedia.org/wiki/Vicipaedia:Legatio_nostra

Low Saxon	1	None
ml: Malayalam Wikipedia Embassy [Malay]	5	http://ml.wikipedia.org/wiki/%E0%B4%B5%E0%B4%BF%E0%B4%95%E0%B4%95%E0%B4%BF%E0%B4%AA%E0%AA%E0%B5%80%E0%B4%B4%A1%E0%B4%BF%E0%B4%AF:Embassy
oc: Ambaissada Occitana [Occitan]	1	http://oc.wikipedia.org/wiki/Wikipèdia:Ambaissada
ru: Русское посольство [Russian]	58	http://ru.wikipedia.org/wiki/Википедия:Посольство
es: Embajada en Español [Spanish]	9	http://es.wikipedia.org/wiki/Wikipedia:Embajadas
uk: Українська Амбасада [Ukranian]	20	http://uk.wikipedia.org/wiki/Вікіпедія:Амбасада
war: Embahada Waraynon [Waray-Waray]	4	http://war.wikipedia.org/wiki/Wikipedia:Embahada_Waraynon

** Low Saxon Request for New Language   http://meta.wikimedia.org/wiki/Requests_for_new_languages/Wikinews_Low_Saxon

** Dutch Low Saxon Wikipedia   http://nds-nl.wikipedia.org/wiki/Veurblad

APPENDIX B: CODING SCHEME

Table 6.5.

Code	Description	Examples
English vs. non-English	Number of English sections (subjects) divided by total number of sections on the Embassy page. Defined based on the language of the first post.	4/16 in English on the Afrikaans Embassy (this example does not provide an accurate number)
NA	No coding on posts that are not in English. Mark NA.	
Writing style (politeness)		
Greetings	Hello, Dear, Hi	Dear sir/madam (English Embassy, Wikipedia Talk page; http://en.wikipedia.org/wiki/Wikipedia_talk:Local_Embassy)
Closing	Regards, Thank you	Thank you With regards (English Embassy, Wikipedia Talk page; http://en.wikipedia.org/wiki/Wikipedia_talk:Local_Embassy) Kit — (English Embassy, Wikipedia Talk page; http://en.wikipedia.org/wiki/Wikipedia_talk:Local_Embassy)
Introducing oneself by name	I am Joe, or sign by name (not Wikipedia user name)	
Content (requesting and/or responding)		
Wikipedia—Information (requesting and/or responding)	Requesting information about Wikipedia pages, bots, policies	"I'm looking for assistance-regarding conflict of interest" in de:Wiki "Photo requests" in de:Wiki I am scottish but I haven't a clue what some of the words used on this site mean!! —Preceding unsigned comment added by Patlawson (talk • contribs) 17:38, 12 July 2009 (UTC) "Kindle Wikipedia"—in German

Wikipedia—Action (requesting and/or responding)	Requesting actions to add links, edit, reorganize, etc.	Add a link to the meta embassies list? It might be a good idea to add a link to (English Embassy, Wikipedia Talk page; http://en.wikipedia.org/wiki/Wikipedia_talk:Local_Embassy/Archive_2) "Needs treaking" OK, I fixed it **Done**
	Responding to request for action and notifying that actions have been taken	(English Embassy, Wikipedia Talk page; http://en.wikipedia.org/wiki/Wikipedia_talk:Local_Embassy/Archive_2)
	Request to rename, consolidate, or change user name	Hi everyone! Is it possible (as on French WP) to rename my account? I'd like t to be Benutzer:TwoWings instead. Thank you to answer on my page. —TwoWings (jraf) 15:47, 28. Okt. 2007 (CET)
	Suggest some actions about how to deal with translation projects	"A way to translate wikilink rapidly" in de:Wiki
Translation (requesting and/or responding)	Requesting translation for specific phrases	Can you translate ja: 旧姓 ソ ー ニ ニ ? I don't know how proper English title should be. But the article explains how a Japanese TV network gathers their national news. —Preceding unsigned comment added by 59.5.206.236 (talk) 09:52, 9 July 2009 (UTC)
	Responding to request for translation	Here is a bad translation that might help.
	Requesting translation for specific articles	(English Embassy, Wikipedia Talk page; http://en.wikipedia.org/wiki/Wikipedia_talk:Local_Embassy/Archive_2) "Translation request" in de:Wiki
	Translation strategies, tools, coordination, etc.	Suppose there are two articles about the same thing, but in diffrent languages, say, English and French. Odds are, the English version will contain more information. Also, many articles that exist in one language won't exist in another. So why not simply create a new article in every Wiki of every language that does not have a certain article by simply using translate.google.com or similar translator? by 69.61.249.178 (talk) 12:55, 18 February 2009 (UTC)

(continued)

Table 6.5. *(Continued)*

Code	Description	Examples
		"GoogleTrans Gadget now available on English Wikipedia" Hello, do you have a translation project on de: (like fr:Wikipédia:Projet/Traduction/Traductions/En cours and en:Wikipedia:Translation into English) ? 81.66.246.77 18:36, 17. Apr 2006 (CEST)
Terminology (requesting and/or responding)	Request about clarification of regional terms	Hi excellencies ;-) , Please, read Wikimedia feedback—Austria & Germany and tell me what you think would be the best method. Thanxalot, Joe
Information (reference questions and answers)	Requesting information about any subjects. It is a reference question.	Now i want a details about "GREEN ENVIRONMENT" articles (English Embassy, Wikipedia Talk page; http://en.wikipedia.org/wiki/Wikipedia_talk:Local_Embassy)
Referrals	Recommendation to ask for help at the reference desk or responding by referring to external sources	I would suggest asking at the reference desk. (English Embassy, Wikipedia Talk page; http://en.wikipedia.org/wiki/Wikipedia_talk:Local_Embassy)
Wikipedia Embassy	Any comments about the Embassy page itself: identify problems, make comments, ask questions, or suggest improvement on the Embassy page	This page is a bit of a mess. Given that it has a direct and static link from the main page, does anyone have any ideas about how we could neaten it up with boxes, better format, layout, &c., &c.? Orthorhombic (talk) 11:53, 27 April 2009 (UTC) No explanation given for why Hebrew needs to be used at the top "MediaWiki Sidebar" in de: Wiki Does this page have a mirror,.....? (English Embassy, Wikipedia Talk page; http://en.wikipedia.org/wiki/Wikipedia_talk:Local_Embassy)

International entries	Comments about topics that are either international or in countries other than English speaking.	"TRUST: What I find still needed about Turkish literature pages of Wikipedia" "Needs your attention"—a case in Indonesia "Wikipedia entry in Chinese on topic . . ." "Dunia and Slovio" in de:Wiki
Real embassy (requests and/or responses)	Messages that confuses the Wikipedia Embassies with US/Canadian/British embassy and ask questions relevant to the real embassies	how do i get a visa please Hi, I would like to visit a friend in Canada, what the requirements? Thanks (English Embassy, Wikipedia Talk page; http://en.wikipedia.org/wiki/Wikipedia_talk:Local_Embassy/Archive_2)
	Responding to individuals who asked questions that should have been asked to the real embassy	As it says at the top, "this page is for discussing Wikipedia-related multilingual coordination." It's not about real world embassies. You might want to ask at the WP:Reference Desk for such general questions, but that's not really an encyclopaedic question either. If you're looking for a visa, you need to talk to the embassy of the country you want to go to. —Amalthea 11:59, 17 March 2009 (UTC) (English Embassy, Wikipedia Talk page; http://en.wikipedia.org/wiki/Wikipedia_talk:Local_Embassy/Archive_2)
Nonsense message	Messages that do not belong to this page. It is either out of context or it appears to be some form of vandalism.	"when i gogle a few friends names it comes uo all about them .who write al this stuff/? "interview skill" "Mrs. Marjorie D'Arcy Stephens"
Internal cross language project	Anything related to a cross language project in Wikipedia (e.g., invitation to collaborate)	"Invitation" "templates needed" "science pearls" in de:Wiki "Adding photos and pending changes / Ajout de photos et changements en attente [Bearbeiten]" in de:Wik

(continued)

Table 6.5. *(Continued)*

Code	Description	Examples
External cross language project	Anything related to a cross language project outside of Wikipedia	"a list of English keywords." (e.g., RU Wikipedia)
Vandalism/copyright violation/blocking users (cross-wiki)	Warning that vandalism is happening in multiple Wikipedias across different languages	"Odd cross-wiki behaviour by someone in Germany; sometimes includes edit-warring and disruptive page creation [Bearbeiten]"
Other	Posts that do not fit into the existing coding scheme, and may require the development of a new code (or not)	English Wikipedia the post about Italian censorship
Cross language: volunteer translation	Volunteer to translate from one language to another	English Wikipedia: "translate button" German Wikipedia: "about Korean Wikipedia"

7

Constructing Local Heroes

Collaborative Narratives of Finnish Corporations in Wikipedia

Salla-Maaria Laaksonen and Merja Porttikivi

INTRODUCTION

The recent advances of online communication have amplified the role of the public and stakeholders in the processes of defining corporate image and corporate reputation. In the online context, the narratives of reputation are formed in various arenas—from news commentaries and personal websites to wikis, blogs, and social networking services. The purpose of this chapter is to investigate how organizations are constituted through participation in a collaborative online arena on the Finnish Wikipedia. Among other social media sites, Wikipedia offers an arena of evaluation of corporations and their roles in society.

Wikipedia is the world-famous open, free, and nonprofit online encyclopedia and is collaboratively updated in 285 different languages. Finnish Wikipedia was opened in 2002, and in May 2013 it contained over 324,000 articles,[1] and on average during the past year there have been 560 active editors and around 105,000 contributions per month.[2] This makes Finnish Wikipedia the nineteenth largest language version of all Wikipedias.[3] Wikipedia has grown to be an important information hub for the web; in fact, the English Wikipedia is the sixth most visited site in the world, as well as in Finland.[4] According to statistics, the Finnish Wikipedia has around sixty-six million page views per month on average.[5] What is further interesting is that during the past few years the amount of active editors has decreased while the number of page views has slightly increased.[6] This is a global phenomenon.

Wikipedia has a unique culture of collaborative editing, shaped by rules and hierarchical structure. The pages of Wikipedia in general are open for anyone to edit, but the process of editing is defined by rules and guidelines. Most importantly, Wikipedia has three core content policies: "neutral point of view," "verifiability," and "no original research." Neutral point of view defines the prerequisite of neutrality as the determining principle of editing Wikipedia. In short, Wikipedia formulates that "editing from a neutral point of view (NPOV) means representing fairly, proportionately, and as far as possible without bias, all significant views that have been published by reliable sources."[7] The two latter policies require that all information published in Wikipedia must be attributable to a reliable, published source—which also means that all material can be verified by later editors and readers if needed.

Different language versions of Wikipedia share common ground. The editing principles described above are common for all Wikipedia language editions, and content is often copied and translated from one language to another. However, as a small language edition with only five million potential readers in Finnish, the Finnish Wikipedia naturally remains rather isolated from readers or editors outside Finland. In general, research has shown that the English-language edition of Wikipedia is the most developed: it has the highest number of participating editors and the comprehensiveness of the entries is much better.[8] However, considering our topic of research, Finnish corporations, it is also notable that likely not all of the Finnish corporations studied would gain equal amounts of attention in the English Wikipedia.

We posit that open and collaborative online services such as Wikipedia create an arena for an ongoing debate about the roles and responsibilities of companies and their activities in society, and more importantly, an arena for discursive definition of the organization.[9] As the wiki platform offers corporate critics an equal opportunity to shape the public image of corporations, it gives more visibility to negative issues such as scandals and failures in social responsibility.[10] In addition, Wikipedia gains high visibility in search engines and is used widely by the public to search and check information.[11] The number of visitors alone makes the service and entry content very relevant considering corporate communications and their reputation management.

Hence, we argue that Wikipedia, due to its participatory and transparent nature, plays an important role in setting the stage for elaborating the interfaces between organizations, their external stakeholders, and the society as a whole. Studying Wikipedia offers insights into tensions, paradoxes, and contradictions in the relationships between organizations and their stakeholders in the cultural context of textual production. In addition, one of the primary features of a wiki platform is the ability to track the steps in the creation of a wiki page. Thus wiki entries are not only purely descriptive texts—via the wiki history tools they also offer insights to the values, ideologies, norms, and technologies behind the text production.[12]

Our aim in this chapter is 1) to demonstrate the ways narratives of Finnish corporations are reproduced in Wikipedia entries, and 2) to study how the conceptions of locality and nationality are presented within these narratives. To achieve these goals, we first discuss previous research on Wikipedia and the nature of its editing process. Second, we present the method and materials used and proceed with the analysis of fourteen corporate entries in the Finnish Wikipedia using narrative theories of Roland Barthes[13] as our analytical framework. Finally, we will conclude with the discussion of these results, and show the ways in which the idea of locality is reproduced and narrated in the process of editing corporate entries.

THE CONTEXT OF WIKIPEDIA: NEUTRAL OR BIASED?

Because of the open nature of the contributions, the trustworthiness and accuracy of the Wikipedia articles has been a popular topic both in media and within the academia.[14] A much-cited article in *Nature*[15] showed that when it comes to the science articles, their level of accuracy is close to the *Encyclopedia Britannica*, but nevertheless inconsistencies or unverified information can be present in the articles at a certain point of time. Especially compared to other easily available websites, the Wikipedia entries in general have been proved sufficiently reliable for many purposes.[16] Another body of research is interested in the behavior and motivation of the active Wikipedia contributors and the social systems and division of labor within the network of volunteers.[17]

Cindy Royal and Deepina Kapila[18] have assessed the completeness of information on Wikipedia. Their results show that a bias was evident, and therefore they came to the conclusion that since Wikipedia reflects the viewpoints, interests, and emphases of the people who use it,[19] it should be viewed more as a socially produced document than a value-free information source. Still, due to the open policy of contribution and content editing, which in some cases may bring on inaccurate, misleading, or generally incorrect information (both purposefully and accidentally), this open policy also enables and generates "wisdom of the crowd." Thus, with many people looking at the content, in the long run accuracy will prevail.[20] This is especially true in cases of blatant factual errors or pure vandalism, which are usually corrected very quickly.

However, this "collaborative knowledge" or the "wisdom of the crowd" has also been questioned. Andrew Feldstein[21] examined the patterns of the collaborative editing process of Wikipedia articles and found that only a small number of editors were involved in the creation process, and only a few members of the large crowd contributed significantly in each individual article. Thus, the widely held conception of the content-creating crowd should be reproblematized. Typically the editing of a Wikipedia article is not a product of democratic, collaborative work, but rather a process carried out by the work of relatively few active contributors.[22] Further, research shows that the time when a contributor begins editing an article impacts how she or he contributes: in the early stage contributors produce content and structure for the entry, whereas at a later stage the edits tend to be editorial work, such as grammatical changes.[23]

Further, studies have shown that the neutrality of Wikipedia is not immune to cultural influences. Ewa S. Callahan and Susan C. Herring[24] analyzed the articles on famous persons in the Polish and English editions of Wikipedia, and they concluded that there were systematic differences related to the different cultures, histories, and values of Poland and the United States. Similar, though less systematic, observations have been made by Josef Kolbitsch and Hermann Maurer,[25] who claim that Wikipedia editors put more weight on *local heroes* and thus create imbalance and bias in reporting. In a larger-scale study, Brent Hecht and Darren Gergle show that the home region of a Wikipedia edition defines the spatial focus of each edition, creating a so-called self-focus bias that occurs when contributors encode information that is important and correct to them but not necessarily from a wider perspective.[26] And finally, Wikipedia itself also admits that the project suffers systemic bias relating to its contributors' demographic groups, the prevalent points of view representing those of the average Wikipedians—technically inclined and educated, English-speaking males from developed countries.[27] Bias takes two forms: articles on neglected topics are scarce, and there is a perspective bias present in several articles.

These notions of bias make it interesting to study on one hand how locality is presented in the Wikipedia entries of corporations, and on the other, when issues related to locality or nationality are not included in the entries. In the context of Wikipedia, the techniques of inclusion and exclusion of facts within an entry are influenced by the user culture (i.e., open editing policy with active individual editors and a hierarchical user structure) and the three core content policies that guide and rule the editors in their creation, construction, and revision of the entries. In our analysis we will examine the enactment of these policies from the conversation in the editing histories. Our attention is especially focused on the core content policy of neutrality. As previous research presented above[28] has shown, in practice Wikipedia pages are socially produced documents with occasional biases. This makes a Wikipedia entry a perfect place to study social conceptions of corporations.

In the history of editing a Wikipedia page, periods of stability and negotiation can be distinguished.[29] Admittedly, most readers are only going to consult the current entry itself. But if someone is particularly interested in a topic, the editing history and the Talk pages can be invaluable resources. For example, one can look to see if there were any dissenting opinions, what these different viewpoints were, and what arguments ultimately survived.[30] In our study, we aim to illustrate this temporal fluctuation by demonstrating the ways in which the collaborative narratives of corporations are constructed of different narrative units. The subject of our study is not individual or group behavior or social structure, but the processes of narration itself.

METHOD

The empirical material for this study consists of the Finnish Wikipedia pages of one hundred top companies in Finland as listed by magazine *Talouselämä*,[31] a local equivalent of the Fortune 500 ratings. The data was collected in June to July 2012. To contextualize the materials, we first focused on the quantitative details of our data. In the first stage of the analysis, we classified these one hundred companies by their Wikipedia coverage using a comparative content analysis of different categories such as presence, entry length, amount of contributors, number of edits, company participation, and amount of debate. Of the one hundred companies in the *Talouselämä* list, eighty-five had a Wikipedia entry, and thus we can report a rather good coverage of corporate entries in Finnish Wikipedia. The average length of an

Table 7.1. Descriptive Statistics of the Data

TABLE 1	Min	Max	Mean	Std. Deviation
Entry length (words)	53	2,156	633.67	493.005
Number of total revisions	5	990	128.21	146.031
Number of minor edits	0	299	45.67	49.479
Number of IP edits	0	365	34.92	49.773
Number of contributors	3	379	56.27	59.546
Average edits per user	1	6	2.27	0.804
Number of references	0	37	6.45	7.861
Valid N = 85				

entry was 633 words, while the range was from 53 to 2,156. For total number of page revisions, the mean was 128 and the average number of contributors 56. See table 7.1 for descriptive data.

Based on a classification of this data, fourteen cases were selected based on our observations and the comments made by Wikipedia contributors in the course of the editing process. We selected cases that had conflicts of interest and editors' expectations visible in their page-editing history. More specifically, the selection was based on two criteria: visible edits and comments regarding corporate crisis, and Talk page discussions on the need to neutralize the entry content. We chose to pick the seven best examples from both of these two categories. We expected these cases to be the best representatives to study tensions related to organizations and the expectations regarding corporations' actions in the Finnish society. Many of these companies are well-known and large Finnish corporations, which is reflected in a more active editing history. In the fourteen wiki entries analyzed, there were 106 editors on average per case, and the average length of an entry was 995 words. See the statistics in more detail in table 7.2.

During the second stage of research the structure of the entries and the process of narrating were studied through the entry history. Here we looked first at the formation of the entry by following the transformations of the structure (i.e., content and headers), and second, at the dialogical process and communication that takes place on the metalevel of Wikipedia, behind the textual level of the entry itself. Thus, for the selected companies, we studied the entire editing history following the trajectories of adding and removing content, paying close attention to the comments and discussions taking place simultaneously. We distinguished all the micronarratives that were building the entry via edit additions, and then classified all the narrative passages using the narrative functions as proposed by Roland Barthes.[32]

Using the Barthesian classification of narrative functional units allowed us to identify the key themes and critical points of the narrative. Barthes classifies the events of a narrative, which he refers to as functions or units ("that have correlates"), to four different groups: informants, indices proper, catalyzers, and cardinal functions. Informants are functions that contain depthless, transparent, and identificatory data.

Table 7.2.   Selected Cases and Their Descriptive Statistics

	Industry	Number of total revisions	Entry length (words)	Number of contributors
Finnair	Aviation	990	2,115	379
Nokia	Mobile Telecommunications	759	2,156	307
Lidl Suomi	Supermarket	384	1,936	189
Fortum	Energy	238	894	83
Valio	Dairy Producer	210	592	92
Stora Enso	Pulp and Paper	201	1,200	94
Neste Oil	Energy	179	1,100	70
Kone	Elevators & Escalators	165	612	91
Eläke-Tapiola	Insurance	122	494	44
DNA	Telecommunications	119	719	59
Uponor	Plumbing	90	612	23
Wihuri	Industry	58	325	19
Skanska	Construction	53	634	28
Planmeca	Medicine	35	536	7

They bring ready-made knowledge, and they have a weak functionality for the constructions of the narrative. Indices proper are functions that might look insignificant but are charged with implicit relevance. Cardinal functions are hinge points of the narrative, moments of risk that occur consecutively and entail important consequences. These are functions that cause the story to change its course. Between the cardinal functions there are catalyzers, slightly misleadingly named moments and areas of safety and rest, which fill the narrative space between cardinal functions. In the context of Wikipedia the periods of inactivity and stability between edits can be seen as catalyzers, and thus are considered less significant in our study. That is why in our analysis we used only three of these four types of functional units—informants, indices proper, and cardinal functions. Whereas informants and indices in the context of Wikipedia can be identified with their content only, cardinal functions are identified by their ability to elicit periods of tense editing that result in a reformulation of the content of the page.

FINDINGS AND DISCUSSION

In this section, we present and discuss our twofold findings. First, we discuss how the editing process of Wikipedia, including editing guidelines and user culture, affects the process of creating corporate entries. Second, we identify how different narrative units build the entries and how issues related to locality are identified within these units.

According to our observation, the process of narrating corporations in Wikipedia is strongly defined not only by the technology but also by the core content policies, editing guidelines, and user culture of the collective platform. Referencing, and the core content policy of *no original research* on its part, contributes to an intertextual network of microstories that create the entry. Additions without sources are quickly removed or marked with a comment "citation needed." On corporate entries the sources used are most often news sites and documents produced by the corporation itself. In practice, and especially related to historical events and corporate critique, this policy leads to the overrepresentation of newspaper sources. Thus, the voice of traditional media is still strong within the Finnish Wikipedia. In addition, our data shows that in the Finnish Wikipedia corporate participation is well accepted as long as the entries are edited according to the core content policies.

The core content policy of *NPOV (neutral point of view)* formulates a prerequisite of using neutral tone and including different viewpoints equally in the entries. In practice, neutrality also means factuality: any emotional or biased statements are quickly corrected back to factual and source-based information. As we followed the process of editing corporate entries, some interesting parameters of defining facts and opinions were revealed. Some parts of corporate stories are taken as facts, such as details related to the corporate history or financial success, whereas more detailed descriptions related to corporate performance, strategy, and especially stakeholder opinions are often contested. Again, regarding the role of news media, it is notable that almost anything published in a trusted, well-known media is accepted as a factual source, whereas if information based on press releases, campaigns, or reports published by nongovernmental organizations is added, the community requires a clear statement of the author of the information.

In general it seems that the Wikipedia community strives to tell a neutral narrative of the corporation. However, over time both promotional narratives and critical counternarratives contest this neutrality. Occasionally, opinion-like statements from the contributors also create bias. The critical hinge points in the formation of the narrative are the moments at which these contesting narratives are resolved. Some traces of these narratives are allowed to stay in the entry, but others are quickly removed. Sourcing, as mentioned above, is one of the key factors in defining relevant, factual, and even neutral information[33]—even to the extent that it can be used as a deceptive tool to increase the weight of a contributor's edits. Nevertheless, the life cycle of fragments that build on opinions only is not very long.

Further, regarding the storytellers, user dedication is strongly present in the editing history: editing of Finnish Wikipedia is largely based on active individual users. For instance, we identified some users who promptly update companies' financial data after each quartile report, and some users who, on the other hand, focus on correcting biased and promotional talk. These specialized users were encountered across the data in almost all of the cases studied. All in all, this is in line with previous research on Wikipedia: there are relatively few active contributors.[34] Previously, the significance of automatic bot edits has been emphasized,[35] but in our data and regarding the narrative construction the bot contributions are playing a minor role: their editing focuses on rather technical edits of updating categories and adding links. This structural work, of course, is important for the Wikipedia knowledge system as a whole, but not that significant for individual corporate narratives.

Narrative Units of a Wikipedia Corporate Entry

A typical corporate entry in Finnish Wikipedia consists of five topical areas or sections: corporate history, info box, financial information, organization structure and business areas, and critique. When the entry is created, usually it contains a short description of the company. Next, the community starts building a picture of the history of the company. At an early stage an info box is added and includes a template-based frame that contains core details and company information, such as company type, industry, location of the headquarters, and recent financial information. Later on some details regarding the structure of the organization are added. These might include details on the different divisions or subsidiaries of the company, corporate governance, or business areas.

Following the trajectory of the entry building, we classified all narrative units the editors added to the entry using Barthes's classification of functional units.[36] A summary of the categories and their correspondents in Wikipedia corporate entries can be seen in table 7.3. First of all, in this classification financial data, organization structure, ownership issues, and the info box data were most often found in the category of informants. This identificatory data was mostly similar for all the companies studied.

In the category of indices proper, a detailed description of the company history and actions was found. Thus, this category consisted of narratives more unique for each corporation. These units included narratives regarding different global or local activities of the company (e.g., Stora Enso's endeavors in Latin America); marketing

Table 7.3.   Categories of Narrative Analysis and Their Correspondents in Wikipedia Corporate Entries

Barthes (1977): functions of a narrative	In Wikipedia corporate entries

Informants
Depthless, transparent, identificatory data
	Company info box
	    Ownership information
	    Financial data
	    Acquisitions & organizational structure

Indices proper
Describes events charged with implicit
    relevance
	Corporate history
	Stories of advertising
	    Success stories
	    National and local issues

Cardinal functions
Hinge points of the narrative; moments of
    risk
	Corporate social responsibility issues
	    Reputational crisis issues
	    Critique

statements and heroic stories of the company actions and deliverables (e.g., Kone elevators' speed records, or the detailed descriptions of Wihuri products and services); stories of advertising (e.g., controversial advertisements from DNA); and significant changes in company strategy (e.g., Nokia moving from the phone business to service industry). Within indices proper we also identified details and descriptive stories presenting the company's activities in Finland and its connections to Finnish society. We named these the "narratives of locality" and will present them in detail in the next subsection.

As cardinal functions of the narrative, we identified units related to corporate social responsibility issues, and also any issues that are contesting the core content policy of neutrality (NPOV), such as editor opinions or promotional tone of writing. Sometimes edits adding details or stories that were considered irrelevant for the narrative formed a hinge point, as they were inflicted with considerable amounts of editing from the Wikipedia community.

The units of cardinal functions together often group under a section dedicated to corporate critique, which was typical of almost all the entries studied in the second phase of our study. Issues related to corporate social responsibility are rather quickly updated below this section as soon as they occur in the news. The critique section is often updated back and forth by a few active contributors who have a clear interest in the area, but at the same time it is a section that attracts anonymous contributors to contribute by bringing details from recent news to Wikipedia. Regarding the practice of corporate reputation management, this section is one of the most important in the Wikipedia entries.

Local Stories

As mentioned above, in the analysis we identified a group of narratives, or a horizontal narrative that we named the narrative of *locality*. Locality refers to details and descriptive stories presenting the company's activities in Finland and its connections and actions in the Finnish society in general. This locality narrative was strongly present in many of the corporate entries, sometimes clearly visible and written out but sometimes hidden between the typical sections of a Wikipedia entry. Most often it was visible in the history section, where the almost heroic stories of Finnish corporations' histories are written out. These hero stories included a company's financial success, elevators' speed records, good sales, the scarcity of flight accidents in company history, or possible awards received.

> The only Finnish Nobel-prize winner in chemistry, A. I. Virtanen, was the director of Valio laboratory for 50 years, and created the tradition for R&D in Valio. The significance of Virtanen's research on silage to livestock husbandry and through that to the whole public nutrition was widely recognized. (Valio, February 7, 2007)

Most locality-related stories are classified under indices proper; thus they are stories that seem unbiased reporting at first but nevertheless carry implicit relevance regarding the story as a whole. However, some locality narratives are also classified as informants. Information such as closing some factories/stores or details regarding stock price are clearly informants, but sometimes they become indices proper through the selection of words.

> Nokia's annual revenue in 2006 (41.1 billion EUR) surpassed the budgeted spending of the state of Finland in 2007 (40.5 billion EUR). Thus Nokia is a very important factor for the Finnish economy. (Nokia, April 18, 2007)

> Only a fraction of the 30 000 employees of Kone work in Finland. (Kone, February 22, 2007)

A few of these informant cases clearly reflect the national importance of the company. The first entry for Finnair (June 19, 2003) was only one sentence: "Finnair is the national airline carrier of Finland." In a similar manner, Valio's importance is reflected in the description taken directly from the company's promotional materials—a sentence that stayed in the entry for almost a year with a label *citation needed*:

> Valio's mission is to secure milk production in Finland. (Valio, January 27, 2010)

Certain locality-related themes were categorized under cardinal functions, the critical hinge points of the narrative. These themes criticize the company explicitly or implicitly and relate to, for example, executive bonus scandals (Finnair), employer politics and strikes (Lidl, Skanska, Finnair), critique concerning high buildings (Kone, Fortum, Skanska, Eläke-Tapiola), outsourcing (Valio), state ownership (Finnair), and company headquarters ruining the landscape (e.g. Eläke-Tapiola, Kone, Fortum).

> Among others the Union of Finnish service workers and its European umbrella have criticized [the company] for its employer politics. In addition, the company's scarce PR has raised upset. (Lidl, April 13, 2005)

> Fortum headquarters is the 4th tallest building in the Helsinki area. It is 84 metres high and much higher than the tower of Helsinki Stadium (72 m). The tower is located by the sea and gives the first impression of Tapiola and Otaniemi areas in Espoo. 68% of Helsinki area inhabitants disapprove high buildings in the area. (Fortum, October 1, 2007)

However, the narrative of locality can have more apparent forms as well. For example, the entry of Lidl, a Germany-based discount supermarket chain, contains— still after five years—a section titled "Lidl getting more Finnish," describing the process of Lidl adjusting its operations to Finnish conditions. This section includes narratives related to Lidl's Central European–style cashier desks, joining the Finnish bottle recycling system, and even the pronunciation key for the company's name.

Hence, the way Lidl is depicted in Wikipedia gives some indications of the distinct ways foreign or global companies are treated in a small language Wikipedia edition.

Another example in which the global villain narrative clashes with the local heroes is shown in the depiction of Valio selling its ice cream business to multinational dairy corporation Nestlé in 2004. The operation raised a lot of public objection due to Nestlé's bad reputation concerning the marketing of infant formula in developing countries. This objection is also visible in Wikipedia:

> Nestlé uses aggressive marketing in developing countries by selling infant formula e.g. through midwives, knowing that the formula will be mixed in contaminated water. Large amount of babies have been killed by contaminated formula mixtures. (Valio, October 5, 2005)

All in all, locality-related issues seem to be a blind spot of the neutral narrating as more loaded narratives are given space through them. Referencing, again, works as a subtle way to leave these narratives visible in the entry in the long run. Only once in our data a NPOV template for representing a local view only was used for the entry of Nokia on December 21, 2010: "This article focuses too much on the Finnish perspective." The template was corrected and removed after four minutes.

CONCLUSION

In this chapter we studied the formation of corporate narratives in Finnish Wikipedia. Our findings illustrate Wikipedia as a multifocal, diverse, and polemic arena for representations of corporations. Analyzing the editing history of fourteen companies revealed traces of individual action, but also a strong influence of the sociotechnical, consensus-seeking system behind the editing process of the online encyclopedia. First, we analyzed how the process of narrating corporate stories in Wikipedia is defined by the core content policies and editing guidelines. The strong policies of sourcing and striving for neutrality create a network of microstories that builds on information from multiple sources both offline and online. In the long run the corporate entries seem to follow quite a similar structure. The information regimes and meaning making of the "offline" world have an effect on the editing process, especially through the use of newspaper articles as a nondisputed, trusted source.

In the second phase we distinguished all the micronarratives that were building the entry via edit additions, and then classified all the narrative passages using Roland Barthes's narrative functions. This classification allowed us to identify which narrative fractions carry more implicit meanings and relevance, and further, what narrative units are the critical hinge points, the turning points of the corporate narrative in Wikipedia. In the course of the editing process the cardinal functions were often grouped under a section dedicated to corporate critique, focusing on social responsibility issues and reputational crises.

The most important classification for this study was the category of indices proper. It included detailed, company-specific descriptions of the company's history and its actions. Within this category we identified a group of narratives related to locality. Some locality narratives, however, were presented as informants or cardinal functions—that is, either as facts or critical issues starting a series of editing. In general, locality-related issues seem to be a passage through which more loaded narratives are given space in the entry.

As a practical conclusion it needs to be noted that Finnish Wikipedia is an online arena with great visibility but with few active users. During our study we noted a clear overall decrease in editing frequency of the corporate entries during 2010, 2011, and 2012, an observation confirmed for the Finnish Wikipedia in general by Wikimedia Stats.[37] Errors and vandalism are still corrected rather promptly, but the content is not developed as actively as in previous years. This means that fewer voices are maintaining this publicity.

Finally, we suggest that more comparative studies between different language versions of Wikipedia and corporate representations should be made. As this study focuses on the Finnish Wikipedia only, it omits any comparative information that could be obtained by including other language versions as well. Thus, in the future it will be necessary to broaden this study to cover other language Wikipedias as well, and comparing the content of the dominant English-language Wikipedia to minority-language editions would be particularly important.

NOTES

1. Finnish Wikipedia, Wikimedia Stats, http://stats.wikimedia.org/EN/SummaryFI.htm.
2. Wikipedia Statistics, Wikimedia Stats, http://stats.wikimedia.org/EN/Sitemap.htm.
3. Wikipedia Statistics, Wikimedia Stats.
4. Alexa, "Top Sites in Finland," http://www.alexa.com/topsites/countries/FI.
5. Wikipedia Statistics, Wikimedia Stats.
6. "Wikipedia Charts—Finnish," Wikimedia Stats, http://stats.wikimedia.org/EN/ChartsWikipediaFI.htm; on Wikipedia globally, see also Aaron Halfaker, Stuart R. Geiger, Jonathan T. Morgan, and John Riedl, "The Rise and Decline of an Open Collaboration System: How Wikipedia's Reaction to Sudden Popularity Is Causing Its Decline," *American Behavioral Scientist* 52, no. 5 (2013): 664–88.
7. Wikipedia:Neutral point of view, Wikipedia, http://en.wikipedia.org/wiki/Wikipedia:Neutral_point_of_view._
8. Morten Rask, "The Richness and Reach of Wikinomics: Is the Free Web-Based Encyclopedia Wikipedia Only for the Rich Countries?" *Proceedings of the Joint Conference of the International Society of Marketing Development and the Macromarketing Society,* June 2–5, 2007, http://papers.ssrn.com/abstract=996158; Ewa S. Callahan and Susan C. Herring, "Cultural Bias in Wikipedia Content on Famous Persons," *Journal of the American Society for Information Science and Technology* 62, no. 10 (2011): 1899–1915, doi:10.1002/asi.21577.

9. See S. Deetz, "Metaphors and the Discursive Production and Reproduction of Organization," in *Organization–Communication: Emerging Perspectives*, 168–82 (Norwood, NJ: Ablex, 1986).

10. Marcia W. DiStaso and Marcus Messner, "Forced Transparency: Corporate Image on Wikipedia and What It Means for Public Relations," *Public Relations Journal* (2010).

11. Don Fallis, "Toward an Epistemology of Wikipedia," *Journal of the American Society for Information Science and Technology* 59, no. 10 (2008): 1662–74; Dirk Lewandowski and Ulrike Spree, "Ranking of Wikipedia Articles in Search Engines Revisited: Fair Ranking for Reasonable Quality?" *Journal of the American Society for Information Science and Technology* 62, no. 1 (2011): 117–32.

12. Andrew Feldstein, "Deconstructing Wikipedia: Collaborative Content Creation in an Open Process Platform," *Procedia-Social and Behavioral Sciences* 26 (2011): 76–84, doi:10.1016/j.sbspro.2011.10.564.

13. Roland Barthes, *Image, Music, Text* (Oxford: University Press, 1977).

14. Jim Giles, "Internet Encyclopaedias Go Head to Head," *Nature* 438, no. 7070 (2005): 900–901, doi:10.1038/438900a; Thomas Chesney, "An Empirical Examination of Wikipedia's Credibility," *First Monday* 11, no. 11 (2006): 1–13, http://firstmonday.org/ojs/index.php/fm/article/view/1413/1331; Fallis, "Toward an Epistemology of Wikipedia."

15. Giles, "Internet Encyclopaedias Go Head to Head."

16. Fallis, "Toward an Epistemology of Wikipedia."

17. Heng-Li Yang and Cheng-Yu Lai, "Motivations of Wikipedia Content Contributors," *Computers in Human Behavior* 26, no. 6 (November 2010): 1377–83, doi:10.1016/j.chb.2010.04.011; Oded Nov, "What Motivates Wikipedians?" *Communications of the ACM* 50, no. 11 (November 2007): 60–64, doi:10.1145/1297797.1297798.

18. Cindy Royal and Deepina Kapila, "What's on Wikipedia, and What's Not . . . ? Assessing Completeness of Information," *Social Science Computer Review* 27, no. 1 (February 1, 2009): 138–48, doi:10.1177/0894439308321890.

19. See also Alexander Halavais and Derek Lackaff, "An Analysis of Topical Coverage of Wikipedia," *Journal of Computer-Mediated Communication* 13, no. 2 (2008): 429–40.

20. Royal and Kapila, "What's on Wikipedia, and What's Not . . . ?"; Fallis, "Toward an Epistemology of Wikipedia."

21. Feldstein, "Deconstructing Wikipedia."

22. Royce Kimmons, "Understanding Collaboration in Wikipedia," *First Monday* 16, no. 12 (2011); Feldstein, "Deconstructing Wikipedia."

23. John Jones, "Patterns of Revision in Online Writing: A Study of Wikipedia's Featured Articles," *Written Communication* 25, no. 2 (2008): 262–89, doi: 10.1177/0741088307312940.

24. Callahan and Herring, "Cultural Bias in Wikipedia Content on Famous Persons."

25. Josef Kolbitsch and Hermann Maurer, "The Transformation of the Web: How Emerging Communities Shape the Information We Consume," *Journal of Universal Computer Science* 12, no. 2 (2006): 187–213.

26. Brent Hecht and Darren Gergle, "Measuring Self-Focus Bias in Community-Maintained Knowledge Repositories," in *Proceedings of the Fourth International Conference on Communities and Technologies*, 11–20 (New York: ACM, 2009).

27. Wikipedia:Systemic bias, http://en.wikipedia.org/wiki/Wikipedia:Systemic_bias.

28. Royal and Kapila, "What's on Wikipedia, and What's Not . . . ?"

29. Fernanda B. Viégas, Martin Wattenberg, and Dave Kushal, "Studying Cooperation and Conflict between Authors with *History Flow* Visualizations," *Proceedings of the*

SIGCHI Conference on Human Factors in Computing Systems (New York: ACM, 2004), doi:10.1145/985692.985765.

30. Fallis, "Toward an Epistemology of Wikipedia."

31. Mirva Heiskanen, "Talouselämä 500: Autokauppa ilman Palatseja—Ja se Kasvaa," *Talouselämä*, January 6, 2013, http://www.talouselama.fi/te500/?view=ranklist&begin=1& end=100.

32. Barthes, *Image, Music, Text*.

33. See also Olof Sundin, "Janitors of Knowledge: Constructing Knowledge in the Everyday Life of Wikipedia Editors," *Journal of Documentation* 67, no. 5 (September 6, 2011): 840–62, doi:10.1108/00220411111164709; Brendan Luyt and Daniel Tan, "Improving Wikipedia's Credibility: References and Citations in a Sample of History Articles," *Journal of the Association for Information Science and Technology* 61, no. 4 (2010): 715–22, doi:10.1002/asi.21304.

34. Kimmons, "Understanding Collaboration in Wikipedia"; Feldstein, "Deconstructing Wikipedia."

35. See Sabine Niederer and José van Dijck, "Wisdom of the Crowd or Technicity of Content? Wikipedia as a Sociotechnical System," *New Media & Society* 12, no. 8 (2010): 1368–87.

36. Barthes, *Image, Music, Text*.

37. "Wikipedia Charts—Finnish," Wikimedia Stats; on Wikipedia globally, see also Halfaker et al., "The Rise and Decline of an Open Collaboration System."

REFERENCES

Alexa. "Top Sites in Finland." http://www.alexa.com/topsites/countries/FI.

Barthes, Roland. *Image, Music, Text*. Oxford: University Press, 1977.

Callahan, Ewa S., and Susan C. Herring. "Cultural Bias in Wikipedia Content on Famous Persons." *Journal of the American Society for Information Science and Technology* 62, no. 10 (2011): 1899–1915. doi:10.1002/asi.21577.

Chesney, Thomas. "An Empirical Examination of Wikipedia's Credibility," *First Monday* 11, no. 11 (2006): 1–13, http://firstmonday.org/ojs/index.php/fm/article/view/1413/1331.

Deetz, Stanley. "Metaphors and the Discursive Production and Reproduction of Organization." In *Organization–Communication: Emerging Perspectives*, 168–82. Norwood, NJ: Ablex, 1986.

DiStaso, Marcia W., and Marcus Messner. "Forced Transparency: Corporate Image on Wikipedia and What It Means for Public Relations." *Public Relations Journal* (2010).

Fallis, Don. "Toward an Epistemology of Wikipedia." *Journal of the American Society for Information Science and Technology* 59, no. 10 (2008): 1662–74.

Feldstein, Andrew. "Deconstructing Wikipedia: Collaborative Content Creation in an Open Process Platform." *Procedia-Social and Behavioral Sciences* 26 (2011): 76–84. doi:10.1016/j.sbspro.2011.10.564.

Giles, Jim. "Internet Encyclopaedias Go Head to Head." *Nature* 438, no. 7070 (2005): 900–901. doi:10.1038/438900a.

Halavais, Alexander, and Derek Lackaff. "An Analysis of Topical Coverage of Wikipedia." *Journal of Computer-Mediated Communication* 13, no. 2 (2008): 429–40.

Halfaker, Aaron, Stuart R. Geiger, Jonathan T. Morgan, and John Riedl. "The Rise and Decline of an Open Collaboration System: How Wikipedia's Reaction to Sudden Popularity Is Causing Its Decline." *American Behavioral Scientist* 52, no. 5 (2013): 664–88.

Hecht, Brent, and Darren Gergle. "Measuring Self-Focus Bias in Community-Maintained Knowledge Repositories." In *Proceedings of the Fourth International Conference on Communities and Technologies*, 11–20. New York: ACM, 2009.

Heiskanen, Mirva. "Talouselämä 500: Autokauppa ilman Palatseja—Ja se Kasvaa." *Talouselämä*, January 6, 2013. http://www.talouselama.fi/te500/?view=ranklist&begin=1&end=100.

Jones, John. "Patterns of Revision in Online Writing: A Study of Wikipedia's Featured Articles." *Written Communication* 25, no. 2 (2008): 262–89. doi: 10.1177/0741088307312940.

Kimmons, Royce. "Understanding Collaboration in Wikipedia." *First Monday* 16, no. 12 (2011).

Kolbitsch, Josef, and Hermann Maurer. "The Transformation of the Web: How Emerging Communities Shape the Information We Consume." *Journal of Universal Computer Science* 12, no. 2 (2006): 187–213.

Lewandowski, Dirk, and Ulrike Spree. "Ranking of Wikipedia Articles in Search Engines Revisited: Fair Ranking for Reasonable Quality?" *Journal of the American Society for Information Science and Technology* 62, no. 1 (2011): 117–32.

Luyt, Brendan, and Daniel Tan. "Improving Wikipedia's Credibility: References and Citations in a Sample of History Articles." *Journal of the Association for Information Science and Technology* 61, no. 4 (2010): 715–22. doi:10.1002/asi.21304.

Niederer, Sabine, and José van Dijck. "Wisdom of the Crowd or Technicity of Content? Wikipedia as a Sociotechnical System." *New Media & Society* 12, no. 8 (2010): 1368–87.

Nov, Oded. "What Motivates Wikipedians?" *Communications of the ACM* 50, no. 11 (November 2007): 60–64. doi:10.1145/1297797.1297798.

Rask, Morten. "The Richness and Reach of Wikinomics: Is the Free Web-Based Encyclopedia Wikipedia Only for the Rich Countries?" *Proceedings of the Joint Conference of the International Society of Marketing Development and the Macromarketing Society*, June 2–5, 2007. http://papers.ssrn.com/abstract-996158.

Royal, Cindy, and Deepina Kapila. "What's on Wikipedia, and What's Not . . . ? Assessing Completeness of Information." *Social Science Computer Review* 27, no. 1 (February 1, 2009): 138–48. doi:10.1177/0894439308321890.

Sundin, Olof. "Janitors of Knowledge: Constructing Knowledge in the Everyday Life of Wikipedia Editors." *Journal of Documentation* 67, no. 5 (September 6, 2011): 840–62. doi:10.1108/00220411111164709.

Viégas, Fernanda B., Martin Wattenberg, and Kushal Dave. "Studying Cooperation and Conflict between Authors with *History Flow* Visualizations." *Proceedings of the SIGCHI Conference on Human Factors in Computing Systems*. New York: ACM, 2004. doi:10.1145/985692.985765.

Yang, Heng-Li, and Cheng-Yu Lai. "Motivations of Wikipedia Content Contributors." *Computers in Human Behavior* 26, no. 6 (November 2010): 1377–83. doi:10.1016/j.chb.2010.04.011.

8

The Copycat of Wikipedia in China

Gehao Zhang

COPYCATS OF WIKIPEDIA

Wikipedia, an online project operated by ordinary people rather than professionals, is often considered a perfect example of human collaboration. Some researchers applaud Wikipedia as one of the few examples of nonmarket peer production in an overwhelmingly corporate ecosystem.[1] Some praise it as a kind of democratization of information[2] and even call it a type of revolution.[3] On the other hand, some researchers worry about the dynamics and consequences of conflicts[4] in Wikipedia. However, all of these researchers have only analyzed the original and most well-known Wikipedia—the English Wikipedia. Instead, this chapter will provide a story from another perspective: the copycat of Wikipedia in China. These copycats imitate almost every feature of Wikipedia from the website layout to the core codes. Even their names are the Chinese equivalent of *Pedia*. With the understanding of Wikipedia's counterpart we can enhance our sociotechnical understanding of Wikipedia from a different angle.

Wikipedia is considered an ideal example of digital commons: volunteers generate content in a repository of knowledge. Nevertheless, this mode of knowledge production could also be used as social factory,[5, 6] and user-generated content may be taken by commercial companies, like other social media. The digital labor and overture work of the volunteers might be exploited without payment. Subsequently, the covert censorship and surveillance system behind the curtain can also mislead the public's understanding of the content. In this sense, the Chinese copycats of Wikipedia provide an extreme example. This chapter focuses on how Chinese copycats of Wikipedia worked as a so-called social factory to pursue commercial profits from volunteers' labor. Due to commercialization, these copycats also suffered more self-censorship and vandalism than Wikipedia itself.

China is one of only a few countries, along with Iran, Saudi Arabia, Syria, and Tunisia, to ban the service of Wikipedia for a long period of time, and thus it acts as an extreme example of global Wikipedia. To date, research on Wikipedia's performance in China has stressed the cultural effects[7] or the proposed effect of network position on the contribution behavior of the editors.[8]

Chinese Wikipedia was established in May 2001 along with twelve other language versions of Wikipedia, a few being Esperanto, French, and Japanese. However, since it did not initially support the proper display of Chinese characters, no content was available. The first Chinese-language page was written over a year later in October 2002. On November 17, 2002, the English article for computer science was translated into Chinese and became the first encyclopedic article. In the later years, the Chinese Wikipedia communities kept working on the conversion between the orthographic representation systems: the Simplified Chinese system used in Mainland China and Singapore, and the Traditional Chinese system used in Taiwan, Hong Kong, and Macau. In the beginning, most articles on the Chinese Wikipedia were translated directly from the English version. By November 2, 2012, the Chinese Wikipedia contained over six hundred thousand articles.

Due to the Chinese government's Internet regulations and policies, the Chinese version of Wikipedia is constantly banned via the so-called Great Firewall. The Great Firewall is officially named the Golden Shield Project, which is a censorship and surveillance project operated by the Ministry of Public Security of the People's Republic of China. The project was initiated in 1998 and began operation in November 2003. Technical methods such as IP blocking, DNS filtering, URL filtering, packet filtering, and connection rest are applied to prevent Chinese Internet users from accessing censored content. These regulations and policies make it difficult for a Chinese Internet user to access the Chinese version of Wikipedia. At the same time, a number of Chinese Internet enterprises have developed their own copycats of Wikipedia, such as Baidu Baike and Hudong; some of them have gained more popularity than the original Wikipedia. These copycats have completely different aims than Wikipedia and therefore apply different policies on editing articles. There are at least two major differences between Wikipedia and its Chinese copycats: first, the copycats are commercial projects even though they claim to be free to use; and second, they apply a censorship system for the submission of edited articles. The system itself is undertaken without public knowledge, as the word *censorship* does not appear in the introductory pages of these copycats, like similar censorship systems in practice by the Chinese media industry.

The first copycat of Wikipedia is Hudong, which was founded in 2005. Later it changed its domain name to baike.com (the Chinese pronunciation of the word *encyclopedia*). As of January 2013, Hudong had more than seven million articles, five hundred thousand categories, 6.8 billion characters, and 7.21 million pictures.

Another copycat, Baidu Baike (or *Baidu*, meaning "encyclopedia"), was developed by a Chinese search engine. Baidu is very successful in terms of the number of articles and number of visitors. After its test version was created on April 20, 2006, the encyclopedia grew to more than ninety thousand articles within three weeks, surpassing the number of articles on the Chinese Wikipedia. On April 21, 2008, Baidu Baike released its formal version. As of January 2013, Baidu Baike had more than 5.8 million articles; it has more articles than the English Wikipedia.

Both Baidu Baike and Hudong claim that they are the largest Chinese encyclopedia. If only analyzing the total number of articles, Hudong might be the largest online encyclopedia in China. However, when examining the number of registered users and page views, Baidu Baike surpasses Hudong.

COPYRIGHTS OF THE COPYCATS

Whereas Wikipedia is covered under the GNU Free Documentation License (GFDL), Baidu Baike and Hudong are fully copyrighted by their owners, and contributors forfeit all rights upon submission to the encyclopedias. Baidu Baike's copyright policy also shows its ambition for a commercial future. In the "terms of use" section of its help page, it states that "by adding content to the site, users agree to assign Baidu rights to their original contributions." It also states that "users cannot violate intellectual property law, and that contributions which quote works held under the Creative Commons and/or GNU Free Documentation License (GFDL) must follow the restrictions of those licenses." However, on the bottom of each page, without a single exception, the copyright information "©2013 Baidu" is displayed, contradicting Baidu's own terms of use. According to the terms of use, either users who publish articles on Baidu Baike or the original copyright holders should own the copyright of the articles on Baidu Baike; however, the copyright "©2013 Baidu" shows that Baidu actually owns the copyright. Wikipedia has criticized Baidu Baike mainly for violating the GFDL. Wikipedia even set up a page listing up to 1,891 articles plagiarized from Wikipedia on Baidu.

In the Hudong encyclopedia, the situation is rather similar. To publish their content, contributors agree to release their writings through a perpetual royalty-free license stating that the information is not free for reuse on other websites.

THE PYRAMID OF EDITORS

To edit articles in Wikipedia, it is not required to be a registered user. In contrast, both Baidu Baike and Hudong require a user to register before becoming an editor. Hudong also allows users to log in to the encyclopedia through other Chinese social media websites. While Wikipedia only requires a user name and password to create an account, both Baidu Baike and Hudong require either the user's e-mail address or mobile phone number.

Another system Baidu Baike uses is the ranking system to encourage user participation. There are fifteen ranks for the users, and credit requirements must be met to increase users' ranks. By contributing to the Baidu Baike encyclopedia, users can earn certain experience credits and wealth credits. For instance, creating a new entry earns five credits for both experience and wealth. Experience credits can be used to increase user rank while wealth credits can be used in Baidu's other commercial services to download documents from its online library. Baidu's online library is a user-generated content platform containing over seventy million electronic documents in .doc, .ppt, .pdf, .txt, and .xls format. In the user manual, Baidu clearly states that wealth credits could be exchanged in another form in the future. Baidu recently announced its own virtual currency scheme, and even though the credit earned in Baidu Baike cannot be exchanged or transferred into virtual currency, users can privately exchange their credits in Baidu's other commercial projects. For example, since June 2012, wealth credits could be used to exchange small gifts in the online Baike Shopping Mall. The gifts range from tools such as nail clippers to an iPod. In this sense, the volunteer editors for Baidu Baike earn a salary; they do not work in vain.

This credit system is more than a monetary reward system. It also forms a hierarchical pyramid, which stratifies the power of editing and modification on Baidu Baike. It seems similar to the system of Wikipedia, although its function varies. If a user's credits are more than 2,500 and 85 percent of his entries have passed the auditing process, he can join the core user team. The process occurs through manual auditing from the editorial team at Baidu. The core user teams chosen from volunteer users are called "tadpole teams" and category editors who need to accumulate certain credits but receive additional editing powers, rewards, or gifts from Baidu, and more privileges such as less censorship. Currently, there are about 150 "tadpole teams." Members of "tadpole teams" have a special logo marked on their ID and their own online workspace in the Baidu Baike personal center page. However, these personal pages are similar to Wikipedia user pages where users can create personal workspaces.

Similarly, Hudong has its own hierarchical system for its registered editors with a more complicated credit calculation system. There are nineteen experience ranks for editors and ten ranks for users based on their credits. Apart from the system itself, Hudong also promotes certain rewarded tasks for registered editors. For instance, in July 2013, users were rewarded for adding items about food and cooking. When editors complete or correct certain entries they are awarded gifts such as an Apple iPad. Interestingly, both Baidu Baike and Hudong use the ancient titles in imperial exams or ranks of nobility in imperial China as their titles for different ranks of experiences or credits.

Blocked Wikipedia and Locked Baike

While we cannot claim that the blockage of Wikipedia in China is an intentional arrangement by the Chinese authority[9] to promote the development of copycats of Wikipedia, data shows that the creation of copycats is related to the blockage of Wikipedia.[10] As discussed earlier, Wikipedia was not blocked when it was first introduced in the Mainland Chinese newspaper *China Computer Education* on

October 20, 2003. Originally, the coverage of Wikipedia was rather positive. The block began on June 3, 2004, which was the fifteenth anniversary of the Tiananmen Square protests of 1989. Afterward, the Chinese Wikipedia refused to restore service with self-censored content. However, on June 22, 2004, the Chinese Wikipedia was unblocked without any explanation, and not long after that it was blocked again. The English and Chinese Wikipedia have been blocked and unblocked several times since then. As of 2012, both the Chinese and English Wikipedias are accessible in China with the exception of political articles. If a Chinese IP address tries to access a "sensitive" article (including searching), the IP address will be blocked from visiting Wikipedia for several minutes. Some researchers believe that the blockage of Wikipedia coincided with the launch of its Chinese counterpart. This has led many observers and users of the Chinese Wikipedia to speculate on the plausibility of coordinated efforts by the Chinese government and Baidu to transfer their actual and potential users to Baidu Baike, be it for political or economic motivations.[11]

During the time Wikipedia was blocked, a "Night Edition Warning" was established in Baidu Baike. The official editor manual of Baidu Baike states that it will not encourage users to spend their sleeping time editing content. Based on this warning, Baidu Baike ceases to update article submissions from 23:00 to 8:30 in Beijing time (Greenwhich Mean Time + 8). In this way, Baidu Baike can use a manual audit process.

Baidu Baike applies a strict censorship system for the submission of articles. The content edited by ordinary users will appear publicly after the audit from internal staff is complete. The audit time varies from several seconds to several hours depending on the rules for different categories. Generally, political issues will be strictly audited. In fact, when editors input their articles, a filter is available that is linked to a sensitive word list that functions like most other user-generated-content websites in China. Any text containing these sensitive words will not be submitted successfully.

According to Baidu Baike, articles or comments containing the following types of content are removed: pornographic, violent, horrible, and uncivilized content; advertisement; reactionary content; personal attacks; content against morality and ethics; and malicious, trivial, or spamlike content. The official explanation attempts to ensure neutrality and avoid disputes within entries, but the details of the rules show the explanation's absurdity. For instance, there is a rule against "hostile attack against government organization and officials." Apparently any negative mention of government officials will be censored under this rule. Similarly, "malicious evaluation of existing national system" is also considered improper and will be deleted.

Even though there is no public list of which articles have been censored, there are several different and well-known types of censorship used in these two encyclopedias. For example, some articles have a locked page with China's official version of information. More sensitive entries are entirely absent from the encyclopedia and China's Internet completely. Generally, those that are absent include highly sensitive events in China's political discourse such as articles about the Cultural Revolution, the Tiananmen Square event, Tibet and East Turkey, and the Taiwan independence movement. The biographies of all the communist leaders except Zhao Ziyang are locked. The article about Zhao either does not exist or users are unable to access it due to Zhao's support for the demonstrating students in Tiananmen Square in 1989. A similar situation occurred for articles about Falun Gong, a spiritual discipline, which first appeared in China in the 1990s and was announced to be a heretical organization by the Chinese government in 1999. There is no public blocking policy; however, there are technical web services, such as www.greatfire.org, that allow users to test whether a website or a web page is blocked in China. If an IP address searches for articles containing any of the so-called sensitive words while visiting Baidu Baike, the IP address will be blocked from the site for several minutes, in a process similar to the Wikipedia IP address block. If there is a list of sensitive words, the list is dynamic and changes according to the situation. In December 2012, before the National Congress of the Chinese Communist Party, articles for Zhao Ziyang, the former Communist Party leader, became accessible through the creation of an official version.

Another category of locked articles has nothing to do with any of the criteria above; these articles are related to Baidu interests. For example, articles about Baidu as a company, Li Yanhong (Baidu's top executive), and Baidu's business partners are locked, so that the negative information about Baidu and its business partners will not be added. Apparently, censorship not only is politically oriented but also operates under a mixture of political pressure and the operator's own commercial interests.

Hudong applies a censorship system as well, but it is slightly different from Baidu Baike's system. Baidu Baike's censorship is used before the submission of an article, whereas Hudong's censorship occurs after the submission of an article. In either case, the users of the online encyclopedia read censored content.

Vandalism and Spoof

Even though Baidu Baike applied a censorship system, which appears to the public as a magic box, users receive their own revenge through vandalism and trolling. Some researchers believe that Wikipedia trolls are one type of hacker involved in creating these problems. The activities of trolls challenge online communities.[12] In the cases of Baidu Baike and Hudong there is no public report about hacking against them, but there are intentional acts of vandalism such as adding and editing spam. In particular, there is a special type of vandalism—some users submit spoofed articles, which involve parody but without revealing its intentions.

Unlike vandalism and spoof, which are equally apparent in Wikipedia, Baidu Baike suffers from less vandalism but numerous instances of spoof. There are intentional spoofs for obvious political and social reasons and unintentional spoofs, resulting from misquotation.

The early media coverage of the spoofed Baidu Baike articles appeared on April 7, 2008. The entry for *Chengguan* (literally the urban management officers) was spoofed because of its notorious reputation for abuse of power and violation of human rights. *Chengguan* was defined as "mafia against the vulnerable groups."

On May 28, 2008, after American film actress Sharon Stone commented on the Chinese earthquake as "karma," the entry about her on Baidu Baike was edited to describe her as a "hooker." Entries such as *civil servant, professor,* and *expert* have also been spoofed based on their negative representation in the Chinese mass media.

During 2009, the Chinese government initiated a special operation against so-called vulgar Internet content. A series of websites were publicly criticized for their vulgar content, and about eight hundred Chinese websites with porn content were closed. At almost the same time, the entry *ten mystical creatures* appeared in Baidu Baike. The so-called magic creatures are actually fugitive animals with names vaguely referring to Chinese profanities using homophones; for instance, Grass Mud Horse (literally means "fuck your mother") and French-Croatian Squid (phonetic translation of "fuck you"). After the deletion of ten mystical creatures from Baidu Baike, parodies such as the "Baidu 10 Legendary Weapons" and "Baidu 10 Secret Delicacies" appeared. Those words were rapidly absorbed into popular culture; even the Internet censorship initiative became a new article in Baidu Baike, River Crab (literally means "harmony").

In the case of Baidu Baike, there are vandals and trolls with a purpose; some of them are highly nationalistic or sexist, as in the case of the Sharon Stone entry. Some, like the case of Chengguan, are based on populism. Spoofed articles like these, and especially those containing political content, were deleted after a media report. The aim of these kinds of vandalism and spoof is not against Baidu Baike, but a symbolic resistance against the censorship system itself.

The spoof and vandalism on Hudong is even worse than what is seen in Baidu Baike. As we discussed above, Hudong applies a censor-after-publication system rather than Baidu Baike's censor-before-publication system. Therefore, the spoofed content without politically sensitive information will continue to appear on Hudong for a relatively long time. For example, some famous spoofed articles still appear in Hudong after media coverage, even after Baidu Baike deletes them. The famous "Grass Mud Horse" is still an article on Hudong as of now with only a minor deletion of direct satire against authority.

The major difference between how the copycats and Wikipedia deal with vandalism and spoof is that there are also unintentionally spoofed articles on Baidu Baike and Hudong. It is not new for Baidu Baike and Hudong to face the problem of vandalism and spoof. However, it is significant that in recent years several reported misquotations of spoofed Baidu Baike entries appeared in the Chinese mass media. Some of them are so ridiculous that it would be common sense to view them as spoof. However, with support from the online encyclopedia the mass media trust the quotes. Some spoofed articles on the online encyclopedias developed into news events. The two most famous spoofed articles are "High Speed Rail Magic Box" and "Yuri's revenge," which are described in the next paragraph.

Since 2010, a parody of the scientific journal article titled "High Speed Rail" has been circulated. It is about a magic box leading to disasters that appeared in a BBS (Bulletin Board System) named MITBBS set up by a group of Chinese overseas students in the United States. In the article, a fictional professor named Zhang Shimai (literal translation of Ten Mile, which is a clear ironic reference to high-speed rail) from the Institute of Earth Environment Chinese Science Academy appeared in an interview and strongly opposed the high-speed rail system in China. Zhang's style of speech imitated a famous opponent of the Three Gorges Project, Professor Huang Wanli. In Zhang's words, due to the so-called *Xiaerxiefu force* (a coined name with Russian pronunciation in Chinese) and the Stephen King effect, the high-speed rail system is extremely dangerous. This article spread in the Chinese cyberworld rapidly and was finally added into the Baidu Baike article for the high-speed rail. The Institute of Earth Environment Chinese Science Academy publicly announced that this so-called professor is not a member of the academy. The original author also made an announcement admitting his improper joke. *South Daily*, one of the leading newspapers, reported these announcements as well. However, there has been no correction or amendment to the high-speed rail article long after these announcements. Other Chinese online encyclopedias cloned this article as well.

On July 23, 2011, two high-speed trains traveling on the Yongtaiwen railway line collided on a viaduct in the suburbs of Wenzhou, Zhejiang province, in China. The two trains derailed each other, and four cars fell off the viaduct. A total of forty people were killed, and at least 192 were injured, twelve of which were severe injuries. An investigative journalism report of the collision in one of the leading Chinese national newspapers, *First Finance Daily*, quoted an article from Baidu Baike (which included information on the Stephen King effect) in their coverage. After the readers of the newspaper reported this error to the newspaper, the part containing spoofed entries was immediately deleted from the official website. After *First Finance Daily's* competitors reported this scandal, Baidu Baike modified the spoofed entries, but as of now Hudong has kept the spoofed article.

A more recent scandal happened on February 2013 in a documentary produced by the National Central Television station about the Prague Spring. The narrative mentioned that the Russian invasion is called Yuri's revenge. Audiences reported that Yuri's revenge has nothing to do with the Prague Spring and is actually part of an extension package for the famous video game *Command & Conquer*. The national station admitted that they referred to Baidu Baike during the production of the documentary. In the historical records of the article on Prague Spring, the spoofed content of Yuri's revenge has been edited several times. Initially this article contained absurd content such as cloned soldiers, which were deleted, but the name "Yuri's revenge" was untouched until mistakenly quoted in the documentary.

The frequent appearance of these unintentional spoofed articles in Baidu Baike and Hudong are attributes of their systems. As we mentioned above, the hierarchical system, commercial rewards for editors' participation, and vague copyright requirements contribute to these issues. In fact, the editors are encouraged to mass-produce new articles. Through this encouragement the chance for spoofed articles increases massively. Some editors even try to copy and paste news reports or other popular content from the Internet to coin new articles for more credits and higher ranks.

Although the auditing policy of these copycats seems stricter than Wikipedia, the auditing focus is only for political issues and "sensitive words." In comparison, spoofed articles that are indirectly related to political issues are easily accepted and published.

Advertisements and Rainbow Products Placement

If the mass representation of spoofed articles is due to the personal pursuit of commercial benefits such as credits and gifts, Baidu Baike and Hudong's potential ambition to commercialize the encyclopedia project is even more suspicious.

There is no hard evidence that Baidu Baike and Hudong insert third-party advertisements in their projects, but there are examples of commercial events created as articles in the Baidu and Hudong online encyclopedias. For example, when searching some typical phrases used in Chinese advertisements such as *welcome to friends* in any of the Chinese online encyclopedias, thousands of entries containing either advertisements or product placement will appear. Even spoofed articles can survive in the online encyclopedia for years. According to its editorial manual, Baidu Baike and Hudong made efforts to ban advertisements within their articles, but advertisements and product placements seek every possible opportunity in these encyclopedias, and publications on online marketing include marketing techniques or search engine optimization skills for Baidu Baike entries. There are articles for companies, products, or advertisements with links in the content or references. It is easy to find a commercial service that adds an advertisement to different Chinese online encyclopedias on taobao.com, an equivalent of eBay in China.

The most controversial articles, with regard to advertisement, appeared in the medical area. According to a media report,[13] on December 6, 2012, an obstetrics and gynecology doctor claimed in his microbiology page that he found the entry for cervical erosion contained mistakes. He spent hours correcting it with his own professional knowledge, but his edition didn't pass the auditing of the official editor. Ironically, a private hospital successfully edited the entry with an amendment of its product placement. In the 185 historical records of the editing of this entry, quite a number of edits were deleted because of advertisements, but within minutes new advertisements were added. It appears that different hospitals deleted the competitor's advertisements but added their own. For instance, the entries for *lupus erythematosus* and *condyloma acuminatum* have long been a battlefield between hospitals.

After the mass media[14] reported this scandal, Baidu Baike officially announced that "Baidu Baike will keep its public service commitment and that all medication entries will be free of any charge."[15] They will promote what they named the Rainbow Project. Under this new project, all the medical entries of the encyclopedia will be locked to general editors. Only registered doctors who are authorized by Baidu

Baike have access to edit the medical entries. There are about forty thousand locked entries. If the entries are edited by authorized doctors, this will be marked on the entry; otherwise, there will be a warning stating "this entry is not confirmed by professionals, the authorization is in the process, and the content is just for reference only."

Ironically, until March 2013, even the entry causing the initial trouble—*cervical erosion*—still contained the name of a certain hospital providing medical treatment. This situation is worse than it used to be since the article is locked under the Rainbow Project and the commercial information within the article cannot be deleted. Another result of the Rainbow Project is that the partners cooperating with Baidu Baike can easily put their own advertisements into the entries. One of the partners of Baidu, Good Doctor Online (www.haodf.com), a commercial website for medical information, has been authorized to publish medical entries under the Rainbow Project and created numerous entries, such as one for gout. Advertisements of hospitals and doctors were placed on the right side of the entries as a part of the authorized information.

Digital Commons or Social Factory?

This chapter does not merely condemn the misuse of the Wikipedia "mode" by the copycats of Wikipedia. The copycats of Wikipedia in China could be considered a typical and extreme example of how social factors change the localization of certain Internet services such as Wikipedia. The challenges that the digital commons face can only be understood through their particular political, economic, and social reality.

Wikipedia is frequently quoted as a typical example of the "shining beacons of a commons based Internet and a political, networked public sphere."[16] What also distinguishes it from other cooperative social media is that "the exploitation of free labor is substituted by voluntary user labor, the profit imperative by nonprofit organizations, the provision of advertising by common knowledge accessible to the world for free, and depoliticized content by a certain degree of political information and debate."[17] Many political economists condemn cooperative social media as a "social factory"[18, 19] while praising, if not deifying, Wikipedia as a "digital commons."[20]

In the case of Wikipedia's Chinese copycats, both Baidu Baike and Hudong keep their distance from the ideal "digital commons" and embrace the concept of a social factory. The products of voluntary user labor are stamped with the trademark ©2013 Baidu or ©2013 Hudong. The limited salaries received by users are exchanged for gifts such as an iPod and iPad.

In some ways, these copycats are even worse than a social factory. A factory pursues profit through exploitation under the market rule. The copycats of Wikipedia keep a balance between market force and political power, taking advantage of both of them.

As an online encyclopedia, Wikipedia promotes knowledge accumulation and distribution. In contrast, the censored articles on Baidu Baike and Hudong narrow the audience's perspective on politically sensitive topics. Again, the copycats' hierarchical system of editors promotes article creation through copy and paste without proper references, while the censorship system completely fails in increasing the quality of the encyclopedia. This chapter describes how incorrect information, originally circulated by the copycat online encyclopedias, moves to mass media, and then finally to the public.

Unlike Wikipedia, its copycats Baidu Baike and Hudong keep most of their strategic plans, such as the details of the censorship system and potential commercial prospects, a secret. We only know a little about their operating mechanisms by comparing the differences between the copycats and Wikipedia. Research on Baidu Baike and Hudong not only increases our knowledge about the political economy structure of contemporary China's Internet circumstances, but also provides a local perspective to envision global phenomenon and challenges the conclusions drawn from taken-for-granted facts.

NOTES

1. José van Dijck, *Wikipedia and the Neutrality Principle* (New York: Oxford University Press, 2013).

2. Danny P. Wallace and Connie Van Fleet, "The Democratization of Information?" *Reference & User Services Quarterly* 45, no. 2 (Winter 2005): 100–103.

3. Andrew Lih, *The Wikipedia Revolution* (New York: Hyperion, 2009).

4. Geertjan De Vugt, "Dare to Edit!—the Politics of Wikipedia," *Ephemera: Theory & Politics in Organization* 10, no. 1 (2010): 64–76.

5. Jernej Prodnik, "A Note on the Ongoing Process of Commodification from the Audience Commodity to the Social Factory," *Triple C* 10, no 2 (2012): 274–301.

6. Chrisitan Fuchs, "Class and Exploitation on the Internet," in *Digital Labor: The Internet as Playground and Factory*, edited by Trebor Scholz (UK: Routledge, 2013).

7. Suo Huijun, "Multicultural Virtual Collaboration: A Case Study of Chinese Wikipedia," 8th Chinese Internet Research Conference, Beijing, China, 2010.

8. Chong Wang and Xiaoquan Zhang, "Network Positions and Contributions to Online Public Goods: The Case of Chinese Wikipedia," *Journal of Management Information Systems* 29, no. 2 (2012): 11–40.

9. Philip Pan, "Reference Tool on Web Finds Fans, Censors," *Washington Post* (Beijing), February 20, 2006, accessed March 10, 2013.

10. Liao Han-Teng, "Wikipedia in Mainland China: The Critical Year of 2005–2008," http://people.oii.ox.ac.uk/hanteng/2012/09/14/wikipedia-in-mainland-china-the-critical-years-of-2005-2008/.

11. Han-Teng, "Wikipedia in Mainland China."

12. Pnina Shachaf and Noriko Hara, "Beyond Vandalism: Wikipedia Trolls," *Journal of Information Science* 36, no. 3 (2010): 357–70.

13. Zhaung Yuan, "Medical Professor Criticizes That Baidu Baike Works as Marketing Tool," *Jing Evening News*, December 10, 2012.

14. Xi Nan, "Baidu Baike: A Business for Marketing Business," *Beijing Daily*, May 31, 2013.

15. Li Bing, "Baidu Invites Experts to Edit Medical Entries," *Beijing Times*, May 22, 2013.

16. Christian Fuchs, "Class and Exploitation on the Internet," in *Digital Labor: The Internet as Playground and Factory*, edited Trebor Scholz (UK: Routledge, 2013).

17. Fuchs, "Class and Exploitation on the Internet."

18. Fuchs, "Class and Exploitation on the Internet."

19. Prodnik, "A Note on the Ongoing Process of Commodification."

20. Graham Murdock and Peter Golding, "Digital Possibilities, Market Realities: The Contradictions of Communications Convergence," *Socialist Register* 38 (2009).

9

Contributing to Wikipedia

A Question of Gender

Hélène Bourdeloie and Michaël Vicente

INTRODUCTION

Although women are more inclined to give—their competence in care, for example, is completely naturalized—they are in the minority both as users of the online encyclopedia Wikipedia and as contributors to its content. In every country, Wiki-Work (participation in the Wikipedia project) differs according to gender—the proportions of users and contributors are much higher for men, who constitute over 80 percent of contributors (Glott, Schmidt, and Ghosh 2010; Dejean and Jullien 2012). As a consequence, this collaborative, nonacademic project has not achieved its main goal: to construct and democratize knowledge as universal and egalitarian. As many works have shown, only a small number of individuals contribute to the encyclopedia, which has been unable to eliminate traditional social and gender divisions (Bourdeloie 2009). Not only are women less common among the contributors, but women (and men) who are uneducated and from disadvantaged socioprofessional categories are also less represented in this community. In this study, among the various determining social factors that influence participation in the Wikipedia project, we have chosen to emphasize the gender issue.

We will start with the observation that the "gender gap" concerns all Wikipedia versions, as shown in the survey conducted by the United Nations University-Maastricht Economic and Social Research Institute on Innovation and Technology[1] (UNU-MERIT; Glott, Schmidt, and Ghosh 2010). Our quantitative study of the French Wikipedia[2] (Jullien et al. 2011)—a research project named Prosodie—showed similar results. We received 13,627 responses from survey participants, of which 5,062 are contributors. Results were published online from mid-January to mid-February 2011. Access was initially limited to a few of the site's organizers, who offered their comments, and then published in the "Bistro" section (discussions regarding Wikipedia), and lastly it was published as a banner on the home page of the French Wikipedia with the collaboration of members of Wikipedia France and administrators of the Internet site. Some 5,139 women responded to this survey; that is 27.71 percent of total respondents. When considering such gender gaps, we postulate that the "gender system," which implies a hierarchy between men and women founded on natural differences, is particularly at cause (Ridgeway and Smith-Lovin 1999). Our hypothesis is that Wikipedia, a "hybrid object"—both technical and cultural—is considered legitimate on the technical plan: highly valued in terms of computer technology but not valued in terms of knowledge, due to its unconventional nature. Indeed, we can recall that the encyclopedia's credibility was highly questioned until the scientific magazine *Nature* published, in December 2005, the results of an investigation proving that the rate of errors in Wikipedia is comparable to that of an official encyclopedia such as *Britannica*. Since then, several scientific works have been eager to show that Wikipedia benefits from a high degree of precision (Chesney 2006). Nonetheless, its informal and nonacademic nature remains. This does not resonate with girls' upbringing regarding culture, as they are socialized in a universe that favors legitimate cultural activities, at least in Western countries such as the United States or France (Octobre 2005; Christin 2012). Inequalities in Wikipedia contributions reflect gender inequalities in society.

LITERATURE REVIEW: COLLABORATIVE PROJECTS, INFORMATION TECHNOLOGY, AND THE "GENDER GAP"

Wikipedia's Characteristics: Uses and Contributions

Wikipedia has been the subject of numerous works, though few question the sociodemographic profiles of either users or contributors. The first consequential survey to have explicitly studied this question is the 2006 international investigation conducted by the UNU-MERIT (Glott, Schmidt, and Ghosh 2010). This investigation is, to our knowledge, the most significant on the subject, generating 125,347 responses, with 24.92 percent female respondents. This study has shown that the majority of contributors are male, with higher education levels than typical users and better knowledge of computers. Even though many factors explain contribution to the encyclopedia, social class and gender, as well as level of education (Glott, Schmidt, and Ghosh 2010; Dejean and Jullien 2012), constitute decisive factors (Lim and Kwon 2010; Lam et al. 2011). This is shown in the results of the international UNU-MERIT investigation and by the Prosodie study conducted on the French version of Wikipedia, whose conclusions were similar concerning diploma and gender variables. Educational background constitutes a significant variable in determining who fulfills the role of contributor (table 9.1). In the case of the French Wikipedia, Wikipedians are even more educated, with a high proportion of PhD users. It has been shown that there is an "entry barrier" to becoming a contributor. This means that even if there is no barrier based on socioeconomic status, the cul-

Table 9.1. Profiles of Users and Contributors to Wikipedia according to Level of Diploma (in %)

	Wikipedia n = 125,347 UNU-MERIT Study		French Wikipedia n = 13,514 Prosodie Study	
	Readers	*Contributors*	*Readers*	*Contributors*
Primary education	14.77	12.36	15.10	12.80
Secondary education	37.69	33.45	22.82	18.88
Higher education—Undergraduate	29.17	28.38	17.90	29.50
Higher education—Masters	10.11	15.07	16.36	21.10
Higher education—PhD*	2.30	4.59	9.49	12.23
Other	5.96	6.15	7.03	5.48

(For the French version of Wikipedia, we based our study on the system of LMD (Licence, Master, Doctorat).

Primary education = before the Baccalaureate (no high school diploma)

Secondary education = Baccalaureate (high school diploma)

Undergraduate = License (three-year college degree)

Higher education—Master = Master

*Higher education PhD = this level of diploma corresponds to the Baccalaureate + six and more, used by the French Prosodie study.

We placed in "Other" those who claim to have no diploma.

tural capital expressed by the educational background constitutes a symbolic barrier. When a larger proportion of contributors have higher education levels than most users, we consider that there is a barrier.

For the UNU-MERIT study, we can situate this barrier at the master's level: 15.07 percent of contributors, and only 10.11 percent of users, have a master's degree (for lower educational degrees, the rate was also lower for users than for contributors). For our study, we can situate this barrier at the level of an undergraduate degree (17.9 percent of readers, 29.5 percent of contributors).

Our study shows similar results with regard to gender, which may constitute a variable determining contribution (table 9.2). Women represent only 12.83 percent of contributors according to the UNU-MERIT study, versus 18.64 percent for the

Table 9.2. Gender and Contribution to Wikipedia (in %)

	Wikipedia n = 125,347 UNU-MERIT Study		French Wikipedia n = 13,514 Prosodie Study	
	Users	*Contributors*	*Users*	*Contributors*
	n = 81,497	n = 43,850	n = 8,486	n = 5,028
Male	68.28	86.56	61.52	81.36
Female	31.23	12.83	38.48	18.64

French version. This "glass ceiling" is not specific to France since it concerns all of Wikipedia's versions (Glott, Schmidt, and Ghosh 2010). As for use of the encyclopedia, although higher, the women's representation remains nonetheless inferior to that of men (31.23 percent in the UNU-MERIT study and 38.48 percent in our study). This gender gap is the subject of our investigation. More specifically, we focus on certain dimensions and on the analysis of underlying causes. Firstly, it is important to emphasize that though the portion of female users tends to increase over time, the proportion of female contributors seems, on the other hand, to stabilize (figure 9.1); it is as if the status of the contributor constituted an obstacle difficult to surmount for women. This leads one to think that the maintenance of a gender gap is less the result of technical inhibitions[3]—that is, a lack of skills—than the result of cultural and symbolic inhibitions linked to gender norms, underlying beliefs, and representations according to which the masculine and the feminine, defined on a sociocultural level, pervade objects as well as practices.

Gender, Computer Software, and ICT

To understand gender distinctions in relation to information and communication technologies (ICT), it is necessary to understand that there can be no biological determinism regarding technology and gender. The microcomputer was, for example, conceived of as an object marked by the seal of male domination (Turkle 1986), although the history of computer programming shows that in the early days of computing we find a significant number of women, although they were only assigned to simple data recording operations (Ensmenger 2010b). However, since

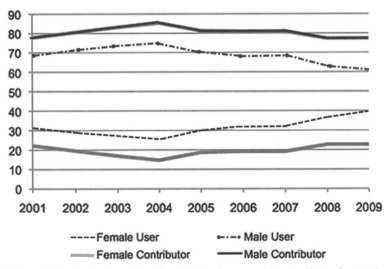

Figure 9.1. Evolution of gender distribution according to date of entry in Wikipedia (Prosodie study).

the time when programming became an industry and a professional field, women have been marginalized (Ensmenger 2010a), especially as proficiency in information technology tests favored masculine backgrounds and characteristics (Ensmenger 2010a, 77–78). This topic is, incidentally, at the core of several works that suggest cultural attributes of male gender were incorporated into computing machines, resulting in women's initial aversion to these objects (Ensmenger 2010a). Indeed, research has indicated that women give up on computers because the software is not appropriate to their gender identity (Perry and Greber 1990). This helps to understand the masculinization of the computing profession (Ensmenger 2010a, 77), why women are nearly always a minority in computer-related projects, why males dominate open source software communities, in which females represent only 1.5 percent of developers (Nafus, Leach, and Krieger 2006)—in contrast to 28 percent in commercial software communities (Nafus, Leach, and Krieger 2006)—and, finally, why those communities are considered extremely sexist (Reagle 2013). There are many causes often found in gender attributes of technological devices. These attributes stem from sociocultural representations according to which computers are not women's business. According to the FLOSSPOLS study, for example, it is shown that women do not gravitate toward the universe of open source software not only because they do not feel welcome but also because the participants in these communities do not generally view their presence favorably (Nafus, Leach, and Krieger 2006).

However, since computers became ICT, with the emergence of the Internet and the digital world, they are attractive to women. This statement is eloquent since it bears witness to the existence of gaps between computer use and the use of media or communication. That is, although computer use has become generalized, there is nonetheless a boundary between the field of computers and that of communication. Computer and Internet use are indeed widespread. Large national and international investigations show that men and women—at least in Western countries—are nearly equal in regard to Internet use (Comscore 2010). Nevertheless, it is not possible to conclude that women's technical skills have increased, in that ICT require few technical skills, but rather, above all, practical skills (Bourdeloie 2013). In this way, it is not possible to interpret the appropriation of ICT by women as a sign of increased technical mastery on their behalf, nor of a valorization of them (Bourdeloie 2013). Digital culture, in the sense that it becomes closer and closer to media culture, does not include any additional prestige, contrary to computer culture, which is a highly valued masculine domain (Collet 2011). This is also confirmed by the fact that computer science professions have gradually become highly esteemed (Ensmenger 2010a).

Possibilities offered by ICT, and particularly by Web 2.0, do not seem to change the stereotypical gender-based division in interests. Studies have shown that many websites reinforce stereotypical representations of male and female roles (Carstensen 2009). In addition, gender-based use confirms the differentiation of activities according to assigned roles: women use the Internet more for communication and men more for information, political news, and leisure (Fallows 2005; Harp and Tremayne

2006; Jones et al. 2009). Works on Wikipedia abound on this topic, including a study showing that men used the encyclopedia more for leisure activities, specifically idle reading (Lim and Kwon 2010). More generally, studies show that gender differences concern not only ICT uses but also the investment of time. Indeed, several investigations highlight differences in time spent on the Internet according to gender, with males devoting more time to entertainment (Fallows 2005; Comscore 2010). The Nafus, Leach, and Krieger FLOSSPOLS (2006) investigation has also shown that differences in participation in open source communities, which require an investment of time, are due to unequal gendered distribution of time: women have less free time because of their participation in domestic and child-rearing tasks (Treas and Drobnič 2010). This is potentially valid for Wikipedia. However, even though gender-based Wikipedia use is influenced by differences in available leisure time, another significant point involves the legitimacy of the encyclopedia. More often than their male counterparts, female students underestimate the quality of references mentioned in the encyclopedia, as if they accorded more importance to conventional sources. They have a less positive image of the project and less confidence in it, as well as in their capacity to evaluate the information presented—that is, in their own skills (Lim and Kwon 2010).

We will now analyze precisely the gender differences judged as the most significant in light of both the technical and cultural nature of this collaborative encyclopedia project that is Wikipedia.

GENDER DIFFERENCES IN WIKIPEDIA'S CONTRIBUTION

In view of both the constant and international characteristics of this "glass ceiling," it is important to understand the inferred meanings regarding gendered relations to skills and expertise. The actual activities performed by the contributors, and the different degrees of legitimacy attributed to these various activities, must also be taken into account.

Gender, Skills, and Expertise

The hypothesis most frequently mentioned in previous studies concerns confidence in one's skills according to gender (Abbiss 2008; Enochsson 2005; Hargittai and Shafer 2006; Vekiri and Chronaki 2008). Confidence is not directly linked to actual skills, but rather to the perception that each person has of their own skills. Several studies have shown that men, without being more knowledgeable than women, tend to overestimate their own computer skills and consider women as less competent (Hargittai and Shafer 2006). In addition, many studies show that young boys have higher self-esteem, especially in their relation to computers (Abbiss 2008; Vekiri and Chronaki 2008), and that, more generally, they affirm greater self-confidence (Enochsson 2005).

Although our statistical investigation does not allow for qualitative consideration of relation to competence, the quantitative results are nonetheless revealing regarding gender. When contributors evaluated their own computer skills, such as the capacity to search for information on the Internet, to conceptualize complex documents, to manage shared files, or to use multimedia skills (table 9.3), it seems that except for searching for information on the Internet, where women are in the majority of those declaring that they have "no problem" (77.7 percent versus 75 percent), and for the conception of complex documents, where the difference is not significant (0.2 percent), for all other activities requiring greater technical expertise, men evaluate themselves higher than women. It is possible to interpret these results in light of men's tendency to overestimate their skills (Hargittai and Shafer 2006), but also in light of the fact that men more often perform the activities requiring the most specific technical skills. Table 9.4 shows that male contributors consider themselves as specialists in a sector (49.9 percent versus 45.2 percent)—that is, in an epistemic space of skills or of knowledge—a situation reversed for the specialization in a type of activity (for example, the activities in table 9.5), where women are the majority (19.8 percent versus 16.3 percent). In reality, these gendered preferences recall the traditional division of roles according to which women focus specifically on identified tasks and men are more willing to recognize themselves as experts and specialists in an epistemic sector.

Gender, Activities, and Legitimacy

Regarding the activities involved in the actual contributions that were catalogued (table 9.5), it is significant that men dominate everywhere except in activities linked to adding references or sources in the text (gap of +1.4 for women [*p*-value: 0.0132]). The result is interesting to observe in that this is a relatively invisible activity—contrary to the proposition of a new article or the reorganization of a text—and one that contributes to legitimizing the credibility of the encyclopedia. The data thus corresponds fully to questions regarding the perception that contributors have of Wikipedia (table 9.6) concerning its organization, adhesion to its philosophy, election process, and more. On this point, there are gaps regarding the "perfectly fair" process of selection and attribution of roles: 14.5 percent of men versus 15.7 percent of women (*p*-value: 0.01188)—and the conception of the tool perceived as a means "important for improving general knowledge" or the adhesion to the philosophy of the project (66.9 percent for men versus 57.9 percent for women [*p*-value: 5.871e-09]). This leads us to the hypothesis that men tend to adhere more readily to the encyclopedia's procedures and mechanisms of legitimization, whereas women appear to be more detached and do not take the project too seriously. In addition, this result confirms the investigation by Lim and Kwon (2010), who show that female students are less inclined than their male counterparts to use unconventional sources of information. It is interesting to view this statement in parallel with works in sociology of culture that show that girls are more encouraged, as children, to exercise legitimate cultural

Table 9.3. Self-Declared Skills of Contributors according to Gender (in %)

	Search for information on the Internet		Conception of complex documents		Management of shared files		Multimedia skills (know how to modify images, sounds, and video)	
	Female	*Male*	*Female*	*Male*	*Female*	*Male*	*Female*	*Male*
No problem	77.7	75.0	56.1	56.3	24.9	29.4	26.2	31.1
Easy	18.0	21.0	29.4	29	25.1	28.5	28.5	28.4
Mostly easy	1.8	2.9	8.7	10.6	27.1	24.5	24.9	23.5
Not easy	2.5	1.0	5.9	4.1	22.9	17.6	20.5	17.0
Pearson's chi-squared test:								
p-value	0.0001114		0.04203		9.858e-05		0.007324	

Reading the table: 77.7% of female contributors consider that they have "no problem" with finding information on the Internet.

Table 9.4. Self-Evaluation of Expertise according to Gender (in %)

	Female	*Male*
Consider themselves specialized in a theme, an area of expertise	45.2	49.9
Consider themselves specialized in an activity	19.8	16.3

Reading the table: 45.2% of female contributors consider themselves specialized in a theme, an area of expertise

activities, with high scholastic value (Octobre 2005; Christin 2012). Women, who participate more than men in high-status cultural activities, are more likely to read fiction, go to art museums, and attend classical and opera concerts, live plays, and dance performances (Christin 2012).

DISCUSSION AND CONCLUSION

In many survey studies, and especially Web-based surveys—a declarative statistical method deprived of face-to-face meetings—the question evidently arises of the representativeness of the sample. However, in basing our own mode of conception and diffusion of the survey on that of UNU-MERIT, we dispose of the methodological means to compare the two studies. Due to similarities concerning level of education, as well as gender and class, the results are important. Another limitation concerns the comparative data gained from the UNU-MERIT study and our study. The later specifically focused on socioprofessional categories of contributors, which were not solicited in the UNU-MERIT study. The French study demonstrates the pertinence of this criteria regarding chief executives (for men: upper classes 27.8 percent versus

Table 9.5. Activities of Contributors according to Gender (in %)

	Female	*Male*	*Gap male— female*	*Pearson's chi-squared test: p-value*
Supplement to a text, content addition	55.5	58.0	+2.5	0.1652
Adding references or sources in a text	29.7	28.3	-1.4	0.0132
Correction of grammar, spelling, or typing mistakes	60.0	64.3	+4.3	0.0783
Clarification of a formulation	28.5	31.6	+3.1	0.06541
Proposition of a new article	21.1	23.8	+2.7	0.07778
Reorganization of a text	15.5	19.9	+4.4	0.001784

Reading the table: 55.5% of female contributors said that they had completed a text or added content.

Table 9.6. Perception of the Legitimacy of Wikipedia

F = Female
M = Male

	A hierarchical structure is necessary for one's performance		You adhere to the overall philosophy of the project		The process of selection and role distribution is fair		You are part of the Wikipedia "community"		Participation in the Wikipedia project is fun for you		It is an important tool for improving your level of general knowledge	
	F	M	F	M	F	M	F	M	F	M	F	M
Totally disagree	5.9	5.2	3.6	1.5	4.0	3.4	15.7	12.0	7.8	7.3	3.6	1.5
Mostly disagree	10.2	9.1	1.2	1.2	3.9	4.0	15.2	16.1	7.8	7.0	1.2	1.2
Neither agree nor disagree	31.6	25.4	9.0	5.3	55.7	51.8	35.2	30.4	15.7	22.9	9.0	5.3
Mostly agree	31.1	35.2	28.3	25.0	20.7	26.3	21.7	28.1	41.9	42.3	28.3	25.0
Totally agree	21.1	25.1	57.9	66.9	15.7	14.5	12.2	13.4	26.7	20.5	57.9	66.9
Pearson's chi-squared test: p-value	0.0002608		1.566e-09		0.01188		2.251e-05		0.0848		5.871e-09	

employees and workers 8.3 percent; in contrast to 23.8 percent and 7.2 percent for women, respectively), as well as students (30 percent male and 27.7 percent female), who constitute a significant proportion of contributors. In the same way, the data that we have for our study allows us to state the cumulative effects according to the level of education and the person's gender. We thus notice that male contributors are always more educated than women, whereas more female than male contributors have no college degree (8.2 percent for women versus 4.9 percent for men).

Limitations must be taken into account: notably, an absence of certain international comparative sociodemographic data. This is due to different methodological tools reflecting cultural factors. Here, we have chosen to focus on gender. We have not added other categories, abandoning an analysis in terms of intersectionality (analysis examining social relations insofar as gender is at the intersection of other power relationships concerning social class, age, race, etc.). Our research allowed us to highlight how gender constitutes a determinant variable for understanding the mechanisms of development of the Wikipedia project. Only a few statistical works (e.g., Liang, Chen, and Hsu 2008 or Antin et al. 2011) have identified the social determinants of participation. On the other hand, Wikipedia has become a field of investigation for numerous researchers who attempt to study the sociotechnological implications of the collaboration. For example, Dejean and Jullien (2012) collected, in 2011, 7,029 articles concerning Wikipedia in the database *Science Direct* (http://www.sciencedirect.com). The majority of articles concerned the analysis of tracks and artifacts. The literature (Jullien 2012) shows us that the questions of users' experience, the quality of articles, and the collaborative structure, as well as conflicts and motivations for participation in Wikipedia, have also been widely studied (e.g., Kimmons 2011; Konieczny 2010). Here, in emphasizing gender, we have attempted to demonstrate that Wikipedia is not an isolated space, but rather profoundly anchored in the social. Thus, as with technical and scientific activities (Keller 1985), participation in Wikipedia is strongly differentiated and largely influenced by class- and gender-based relations of domination. The latter are manifested in various ways: by the underrepresentation of collaboration and use by women, so that the production of "female content" constitutes a real challenge for the Wikimedia Foundation (Bourdeloie 2013). Finally, the Wikipedia project contributes to maintaining the gender system, "which includes processes that both define males and females as different in socially significant ways and justify inequalities on the basis of that difference" (Ridgeway and Smith-Lovin 1999), even if it offers possibilities for displacing the gendered lines dividing activities.

NOTES

1. Led by the UNU-MERIT (center for research and study at the University of the United Nations and the University of Maastricht in the Netherlands) at the request of the Wikimedia Foundation, the international investigation on Wikipedia's readers and contributors (the

Wikipedia Survey) was translated and published online during the second trimester of 2008 in over twenty languages.

2. This survey was conducted in the context of the ANR CCCP-Prosodie Program (2009–2012).

3. For example, the UNU-MERIT study (Glott, Schmidt, and Ghosh 2010) has shown that only 8 percent of respondents would be more inclined to contribute to the online encyclopedia if "the technology were easier to use."

REFERENCES

Abbiss, Jane. 2008. "Rethinking the 'Problem' of Gender and IT Schooling: Discourse in Literature." *Gender and Education* 20, no. 2: 153–65.

Antin, Judd, Raymond Yee, Coye Cheshire, and Oded Nov. 2011. "Gender Differences in Wikipedia Editing." In *WikiSym 2011 Conference Proceedings—7th Annual International Symposium on Wikis and Open Collaboration*, 11–14.

Bourdeloie, Hélène. 2009. "Ressources Ouvertes, Construction Coopérative de la Connaissance et Fracture Numérique. Le Cas de l'Encyclopédie en Ligne Wikipédia." In *Fractures, mutations, fragmentations: de la diversité des cultures numériques*, edited by Alain Kiyindou, 195–224. London: Hermès Lavoisier.

———. 2013. "Expressive Digital Media and Social Relations of Gender and Class." In *La Communication électronique en questions*, edited by Sami Zlitni and Fabien Liénard, 253–66. Bern: Peter Lang.

Carstensen, Tanja. 2009. "Gender Trouble in Web 2.0: Gender Relations in Social Network Sites, Wikis and Weblogs." *International Journal of Gender, Science and Technology* 1, no. 1: 106–27.

Chesney, Thomas. 2006. "An Empirical Examination of Wikipédia's Credibility." *First Monday* 11. http://www.firstmonday.org/htbin/cgiwrap/bin/ojs/index.php/fm/article/view/1413/1331.

Christin, Angèle. 2012. "Gender and Highbrow Cultural Participation in the United States." *Poetics* 40, no. 5: 423–43.

Collet, Isabelle. 2011. "Effet de Genre: le Paradoxe des Études d'Informatique." *Tic&société* 5, no. 1. http://ticetsociete.revues.org/955.

Comscore. 2010. "Women on the Web: How Women Are Shaping the Internet." http://www.iab.net/media/file/womenontheweb.pdf.

Dejean, Sylvain, and Nicolas Jullien. 2012. "Enrolled since the Beginning: Assessing Wikipedia Contributors' Behavior by Their First Contribution." http://papers.ssrn.com/sol3/papers.cfm?abstract_id=1980806.

Enochsson, Ann B. 2005. "A Gender Perspective on Internet Use: Consequences for Information Seeking." *Information Research* 10, no. 4. http://informationr.net/ir/10-4/paper237.

Ensmenger, Nathan. 2010a. *The Computer Boys Take Over: Computers, Programmers and the Politics of Technical Expertise*. Cambridge: MIT Press, 2010a.

———. 2010b. "Making Programming Masculine." In *Gender Codes: Why Women Are Leaving Computing*, edited by Thomas J. Misa. Hoboken, NJ: Wiley.

Fallows, Deborah. 2005. "How Women and Men Use the Internet." http://www.pewinternet.org/Reports/2005/How-Women-and-Men-Use-the-Internet.aspx.

Flanagin, Andrew J., and Miriam J. Metzger. 2011. "From Encyclopædia Britannica to Wikipedia: Generational Differences in the Perceived Credibility of Online Encyclopedia Information." *Information Communication and Society* 14, no. 3 (2011): 355–74.

Forte, Andrea, and Amy Bruckman. 2005. "Why Do People Write for Wikipedia? Incentives to Contribute to Open-Content Publishing." Paper presented at GROUP Conference (November 6–9, 2005), Sanibel Island, Florida. http://www.andreaforte.net/ForteBruck manWhyPeopleWrite.pdf.

Gardey, Delphine. 2001. "Mechanizing Writing and Photographing the Word: Utopias, Office Work, and Histories of Gender and Technology." *History and Technology* 17, no. 4: 319–52.

Glott, Ruediger, Philipp Schmidt, and Rishab Ghosh. 2010. "Wikipedia Survey. Overview of Results." United Nations University UNU-MERIT. http://www.Wikipédiasurvey.org/docs/ Wikipédia_Overview_15March2010-FINAL.pdf.

Hargittai, Eszter, and Steven Shafer. 2006. "Differences in Actual and Perceived Online Skills: The Role of Gender." *Social Science Quarterly* 87, no. 2 (2006): 432–48.

Harp, Dustin, and Mark Tremayne. 2006. "The Gendered Blogosphere: Examining Inequality Using Network and Feminist Theory." *Journalism and Mass Communication Quarterly* 83, no. 2 (2006): 247–64.

Jones, Steve, Camille Johnson-Yale, Sarah Millermaier, and Francisco S. Pérez. 2009. "U.S. College Students' Internet Use: Race, Gender and Digital Divides." *Journal of Computer-Mediated Communication* 14: 244–64. http://www3.interscience.wiley.com/cgi-bin/full text/122295227/HTMLSTART.

Jullien, Nicolas. 2012. "What We Know about Wikipedia. A Review of the Literature Analyzing the Project(s)." http://papers.ssrn.com/sol3/papers.cfm?abstract_id=2053597.

Jullien, Nicolas, Roudaut Karine, Dejean Sylvain, Lyubareva Inna, and Vicente Michaël. 2011. "Etude sur les utilisateurs et les contributeurs de Wikipédia." *Cahier de recherche Marsouin*, no 4. http://www.marsouin.org/spip.php?article 452.

Keller, Evelyn Fox. 1985. *Reflections on Gender and Science*. New Haven, CT: Yale University Press, 1985.

Kimmons, Royce. 2011. "Understanding Collaboration in Wikipedia." *First Monday* 16, no. 12. http://firstmonday.org/article/view/3613/3117.

Konieczny, Piotr. 2010. "Adhocratic Governance in the Internet Age: A Case of Wikipedia." *Journal of Information Technology and Politics* 7, no. 4: 263–83.

Lam, Shyong K., Anuradha Uduwage, Zhenhua Dong, Shilad Sen, David R. Musicant, Loren Terveen, and John Riedl. 2011. "WP:Clubhouse? An Exploration of Wikipedia's Gender Imbalance." In *Proceedings of the 7th International Symposium on Wikis and Open Collaboration*, WikiSym'11. New York: ACM. http://grouplens.org/system/files/wp-gender -wikisym2011.pdf.

Liang, Chao-Yun, Chia-Heng Chen, and Yu-Ling Hsu. 2008. "The Participation Motivation and Work Styles of the Administrators for Chinese Wikipedia." *Journal of Educational Media and Library Science* 46, no. 1: 81–110.

Lim, Sook, and Nahyun Kwon. 2010. "Gender Differences in Information Behavior Concerning Wikipedia, an Unorthodox Information Source?" *Library and Information Science Research* 32, no. 3: 212–20.

Nafus, Dawn, James Leach, and Bernhard Krieger. 2006. "FLOSSPOLS, Free/Libre and Open Source Software: Policy Support, Gender: Integrated." Report of Findings, Cambridge. http://flosspols.org/deliverables/FLOSSPOLS-D16-Gender_Integrated_Report_ of_Findings.pdf.

Niederle, Muriel, and Lise Vesterlund. 2007. "Do Women Shy Away from Competition? Do Men Compete Too Much?" *Quarterly Journal of Economics* 122, no. 3: 1067–1101.

Octobre, Sylvie. 2005. "La fabrique sexuée des goûts culturels." *Développement Culturel*, no. 150. http://www.culture.gouv.fr/culture/editions/r-devc/dc150.pdf.

Perry, Ruth, and Lisa Greber. 1990. "Women and Computers: An Introduction." *Signs* 16, no. 1: 74–101.

Reagle, Joseph. 2013. "'Free As in Sexist?': Free Culture and the Gender Gap." *First Monday* 18, no. 1. http://www.firstmonday.org/htbin/cgiwrap/bin/ojs/index.php/fm/article/view/4291/3381.

Ridgeway, Cecilia L., and Lynn Smith-Lovin. 1999. "The Gender System and Interaction." *Annual Review of Sociology* 25: 191–216.

Treas, Judith, and Sonja Drobnič, eds. 2010. "Dividing the Domestic: Men, Women, and Household Work in Cross-National Perspective." In *Studies in Social Inequality*. Stanford, CA: Stanford University Press.

Turkle, Sherry. 1986. "Computational Reticence: Why Women Fear the Intimate Machine." In *Technology and Women's Voices*, edited by Cheris Kramarae, 41–61. New York: Pergamon Press.

Vekiri, Ioanna, and Anna Chronaki. 2008. "Gender Issues in Technology Use: Perceived Social Support, Computer Self-Efficacy and Value Beliefs, and Computer Use Beyond School." *Computers and Education*, no. 51: 1392–1404.

Index

About the Editors and Contributors

Hélène Bourdeloie is associate professor at Université Paris 13—Sorbonne Paris Cité, LabSic—Labex ICCA and Research Associate in the laboratory Costech (UTC). She conducts research on cultural practices and the uses of digital information and communication. Her current research focuses on the practice of digital writing and investigates the question of gender.

Ewa Callahan is associate professor of Communications at Quinnipiac University. She holds a PhD in information science from Indiana University, as well as an MA in history from Jagiellonian University in Krakow, Poland. Dr. Callahan's teaching and research interests relate mainly to the areas of international and intercultural communication, social informatics, children and media, scholarly communication, and human-computer interaction. She has published articles in journals such as the *Annual Review of Information Science and Technology*, the *Journal of Computer-Mediated Communication*, the *International Journal of Communication*, and the *Journal of the American Society for Information Science and Technology*, and she actively presents at national and international conferences.

Pnina Fichman is associate professor in the School of Informatics and Computing, the director of the Rob Kling Center of Social Informatics, and the chair of the Department of Information and Library Science at Indiana University Bloomington. She earned her PhD from the University of North Carolina. Her research in social informatics focuses on the interaction between ICTs and cultural diversity in online communities and virtual teams, online deviant behaviors, such as trolling and discrimination. In addition to her two books, *Social Informatics: Past Present and Future* and *Multiculturalism and Information and Communication Technology*, her publications have appeared in *Information and Management*, the *Journal of the American*

Society for Information Science & Technology, the *Journal of Information Science*, and other venues.

Mark Graham (http://www.oii.ox.ac.uk/people/graham/) is director of research at the Oxford Internet Institute and a visiting research associate at the University of Oxford's School of Geography and the Environment. He conducts research on Internet geography, user-generated content, and the geographies of knowledge.

Noriko Hara is an associate professor in the School of Informatics and Computing at Indiana University-Bloomington. Her research examines the means by which collective behaviors—including knowledge sharing, online mobilization, and communities of practice—are enabled and/or impeded by information technology and is rooted in the social informatics perspective. She is the author of *Communities of Practice: Fostering Peer-to-Peer Learning and Informal Knowledge Sharing*. Her publications have appeared in the *Journal of the American Society for Information Science and Technology*; *Information, Communication & Society*; the *Information Society*; and *Instructional Science*, among others.

János Kertész (http://www.phy.bme.hu/~kertesz/) is full professor at the Central European University and at the Budapest University of Technology and Economics. He has broad experience in statistical physics and its applications. His research focuses on multidisciplinary topics, mainly on complex networks and human behavior, with top-tier publications in these fields.

Salla-Maaria Laaksonen (MSocSc) is a doctoral candidate and a project researcher at the Department of Social Research (Media and Communication Studies) in the University of Helsinki. Her doctoral dissertation focuses on how corporate reputations are narrated in digital public spaces, looking at the process of reputation creation and management on the levels of individuals, organizations, and narrative content. Her other areas of research include studying corporate-related emotions using experimental methods and political communication in social media.

Randall Livingstone is assistant professor in the School of Communication at Endicott College. He earned his PhD from the School of Journalism and Communication at the University of Oregon, where his dissertation work focused on the sociotechnical nature of Wikipedia. His work on new media and other areas of mass media has appeared in the *Journal of Communication Inquiry*, *M/C Journal*, *FLOW*, and the *Newspaper Research Journal*.

Paolo Massa is a researcher at IRST (Institute for Scientific and Technological Research) at the Bruno Kessler Foundation (FBK) in Trento, Italy, where he works in the I3 (Intelligent Interfaces & Interaction) research group. He received his PhD from ICT International Graduate School of University of Trento in March 2006, defending a thesis titled "Trust-Aware Decentralized Recommender Systems." Paolo's research interests include trust and reputation, recommender systems, and commons-based peer production phenomena such as Wikipedia. A list of his publications is available at http://www.gnuband.org.

Jahna Otterbacher (PhD, University of Michigan-Ann Arbor) teaches communication and social computing at the Open University of Cyprus. Her research focuses on interactions between people in technology-mediated environments in which the primary mode of communication is written text. She views writing as a social interaction, in that what and how one writes create an impression as to one's personality and credibility as a source of information. She uses mixed methodologies in her research, including quantitative and textual analyses. Her endeavor is to discover patterns in the use of language and other communicative devices in order to better facilitate interactions between people, enhancing their access to information.

Merja Porttikivi (M Sc Econ) is a doctoral candidate in the Department of the Communication in Aalto University School of Business. She is currently finalizing her PhD thesis on "Civic Engagement in Online Public Sphere." Her doctoral dissertation focuses on the potential of a new and still emerging online public sphere, and it illustrates how the special features and practices of online interaction disclose different multiple and counterhegemonic voices. Her research interests include critical and discursive perspectives on Corporate Social Responsibilty, the role of online media in participatory democracy, and the genre and practices of online discussion.

Anselm Spoerri (http://comminfo.rutgers.edu/~aspoerri/) is a lecturer/assistant professor at the School of Information and Communication at Rutgers University, where he teaches and conducts research in the areas of information visualization, data fusion, and multimedia interfaces.

Michaël Vicente is associate professor at the University of Technology of Compiègne (UTC), Costech. He conducts research on digital content producers. His previous work focused on free software developer communities.

Taha Yasseri (http://www.oii.ox.ac.uk/people/yasseri/) is a research officer at the Oxford Internet Institute, University of Oxford. Prior to this, he (as a physicist by training) has been working on the social aspects of Wikipedia editors' community with a focus on conflict and cooperation during his two years postdoc at the Department of Physics, Budapest University of Technology and Economics.

Asta Zelenkauskaite is an assistant professor of communication in the Department of Culture and Communication at Drexel University. She earned her doctoral degree (PhD) in mass communication from Indiana University-Bloomington. Her main research areas focus on the ways in which communication practices are shaped by new communication technologies such as computer network environments. She is also interested in the collaborative process in online environments. Dr. Zelenkauskaite researches these phenomena from a multimethod approach, including computer-mediated discourse analysis, social network analysis, and content analysis. Her research has been featured in *Written Communication*, the *Journal of Communication*, the *Newspaper Research Journal*, and the *Journal of Broadcasting and Electronic Media*.

Gehao Zhang is associate professor at Macau University of Science and Technology, with a PhD in media and cultural analysis from Loughborough University, United Kingdom. His main research interests are the political economy of culture, cultural studies, and computer-assisted qualitative data analysis.